• • •

Dishing with Kathy Casey

Dishing

with Kathy Casey

• • •

Food, Fun &

Cocktails from Seattle's

Culinary Diva

Photographs by
E. Jane Armstrong

 SASQUATCH BOOKS
SEATTLE

Printed in China
Distributed by Publishers Group West
09 08 07 06 05 04 03 02   7 6 5 4 3 2 1

Cover and interior design: Karen Schober
Cover and interior photographs: E. Jane Armstrong
Food styling: Kathy Casey and Charlotte Rudge
Interior composition: Kate Basart
Copy editor: Rebecca Pepper
Proofreader: Sigrid Asmus
Indexer: Miriam Bulmer

Library of Congress Cataloging in Publication Data
Casey, Kathy.
Dishing with Kathy Casey : food, fun, and cocktails from Seattle's culinary diva /
by Kathy Casey; photography by E. Jane Armstrong.
          p.   cm.
1. Cookery. 2. Menus. I. Title.

TX714 .C3749 2002
641.5—dc21

Sasquatch Books
615 Second Avenue
Seattle, Washington 98104
(206) 467-4300
books@SasquatchBooks.com
http://www.SasquatchBooks.com

• • •

CONTENTS

vii   Acknowledgments

viii   Introduction

Menus   **1**

Sips   **27**

Teasers   **49**

Starters   **77**

Mains   **99**

Sides   **127**

Comforts   **151**

Sweets   **171**

202   Index

212   About the Photographer

213   About the Author

I would like to dedicate this book to John Casey, my husband and always-willing partner in my never-ending culinary adventures.

• • •

Acknowledgments

In cooking it's not just one "thing" that makes a great dish or meal. In the same way, a cookbook cannot be created or "cooked up" alone, but takes the talents, tribulations, and trials of many. I would like to thank my husband, John Casey, who is chief taste-tester and stress-calmer; my longtime associate, Ann Manly, for her superb recipe editing expertise; sous-chef Charlotte Rudge, for her delicious testing talent and food styling assistance; my business manager, Liv Fagerholm, for organizing everything and everybody, all the while editing like mad; Sasquatch Books editor Suzanne De Galan, for her creative insights, gentle prodding, skillful editing, and attention to quality; art director Karen Schober, for her beautiful design; and the rest of the Sasquatch team for its enthusiasm and dedication to this book. As always, thank you, Tamara Wilson, for being my gal pal, publicist, and PR queen. And last but most definitely not least, I thank my good friend and brilliant photographer, E. Jane Armstrong, for bringing the beauty of food to life on these pages.

I have always loved to cook—from my early years of baking fluorescent blue and green frosted cookies, to culinary school, to my early tenure as executive chef at Seattle's Fullers, where I helped bring Northwest cuisine to national attention. It was all of these experiences that led me to where I am today, consulting on restaurant concepts, menus, and food products for others. Developing new recipes, predicting trends, and exercising my culinary creativity is so much fun that sometimes I can't believe it is my job and that I get paid for it!

● ● ●

Introduction

People ask me how I come up with recipes and dishes. Well it just comes naturally to me. And, like a lot of creative people, I "cook" up the best ideas right before falling asleep. I might be inspired by something I saw—a new ingredient, a city, a country, even a color or shape—or something I have eaten somewhere else. Inspiration comes from everywhere.

This year I opened Kathy Casey Food Studios® to the public, with classes, special dinners, and events. What a pleasure it is to be sharing what I have always loved to do, and how gratifying it is when people come back and tell me what great success they had re-creating a dinner I had taught them!

My style of cooking is what I try to teach others: Be fearless and go for it. The most important thing to remember is that if you don't try something, you'll never know how great it could have been. But experiment with food on yourself—don't be serving new creations to a big party! And don't let flops discourage you; everyone has them, even chefs.

In this book I have included recipes you can feel confident about preparing, from simple, easy comfort foods, super-fun appetizers, and lively libations, to more complicated main dishes with multiple components . . . and, of course, lots of scrumptious desserts. After all, even if you're equipped with great foodie instincts and armed with fabulous taste sensibilities, it never hurts to have a great recipe.

Cooking should be a joy, not a daunting task. It brings us together around the table for great food and drink and the company of friends. It gets us conversing, laughing, and sharing with each other. From a multicourse sit-down to a lively sip-and-nibble cocktail party to a patio potluck, dinner parties are back. And I have included a whole chapter on Menus for these occasions to take the guesswork out of putting it all together.

So get cooking and creating, and enjoy this cookbook. I wish you many wonderful culinary adventures.

Cook up some fun!®

—Kathy Casey

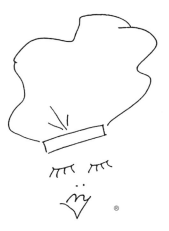

• • •

MENUS

Romantic Dinner

Dinner Party with Friends

First Taste of Summer Celebration

Pacific Rim Party

Fabulous Fall Dinner for Six

Posh Patio "Picnic"

Remembering Sunday Dinner

New Classics Cocktail Party

Fiesta with Friends

Inexpensive Fancy Pants "Faux French" Dinner

Surprise Breakfast in Bed

The Big Holiday Feast

"Share the Work" Summer Entertaining

Simple Summer Supper

Tiki Torch Dreamin'

Autumn Fireside Dinner

Somewhere between the invention of the microwave and the growing sixty-hour workweek, entertaining at home has become an endangered art. And yet, what better way to reconnect with friends and family than over the dinner table, sharing great conversation, food, and drink?

• • •

Making a Menu

Putting together a great party can be daunting and, to say the least, quite stressful. But it really doesn't have to be if you have thought it out—not just the food, but the whole shebang: dishes, silverware, glasses, what to drink.

For the uninitiated party giver, the tricks are: Don't over-do and don't be intimidated.

You would think that, as a professional chef well versed in "dining," I would have known this. About ten years ago, however, I orchestrated what turned out to be a nightmare dinner party: I insisted on sewing my own napkins, creating the napkin rings and centerpiece, hand-lettering and painting the menus, and cooking up eight courses in my "quaint" kitchen that had lots of charm but not lots of anything else. I lived in the kitchen for five days, making bread, desserts, rolls, cookies, candy, a barrage of appetizers, and, of course, a fancy-pants entrée.

Needless to say I did *not* enjoy my own party. Even before the first appetizer was served I was exhausted. Nor did I enjoy washing every single dish and pan I owned the next day . . . in the bathtub!

Today I try to practice and preach "casual elegance"—it can be achieved within a tight budget or by spending lots of cash.

For starters, figure out your menu. Have a mix of simple dishes and one or two more challenging ones. Consider what item will be cooked where. For instance, don't plan on baking rolls at the same time you've got a roast in the oven, because they will probably cook at different temperatures. When having appetizers, serve one item that's hot and a couple of cold ones, at least one of those being something that can be cooked in advance and served chilled.

I've put together the menus in this chapter to illustrate these principles. Depending on your culinary experience, you may want to try one or all of the dishes recommended in any given menu. But you should feel free to substitute here or there with simple steamed vegetables or green salad, or with a tried-and-true favorite dish.

Print out your recipe for each course and list every component that's going on each plate. Put a star beside what needs to be prepped and determine what you can make ahead of time. For example, you can usually make salad dressing a couple of days ahead, then clean and spin the greens the evening before and keep them in a plastic bag. For dessert served with a sauce, you can usually prepare the sauce in advance and have it ready in a squirt bottle.

If a dish's presentation is complicated, draw a diagram of it. List the plate ware and silverware needed for each course, and whether a serving utensil will be needed. Pull out and count the plates you are going to use for each course and chill them ahead of time or have them ready to go and just pop in the oven to warm right before serving. I like to have all my bowls and pots out, lined up by course. This way I'll hopefully never forget a thing.

If you have a heavy work schedule, who says you can't get the dining room set up days before? Even if you are just planning a dinner for two to six people, be prepared and organized, and set the table ahead if you can. Make a general timeline of what you're doing and when.

A great-looking table doesn't have to be all prim and proper, but it does require a few indispensables. You will need lots of flatware, but don't worry about it all matching. A mix-and-match look can be quite charming, especially if you use actual *silver* silverware. Pre-setting for each course looks elegant and is easier for service. I like to collect dishes with certain characteristics that tie them together—for example, a gold rim, or fleur-de-lis pattern trim. White is my favorite color for dishware—you can't go wrong with classic white or bone. A few fine porcelain formal dishes can be mixed in with more casual pieces. Look for different sizes and shapes to add variety.

If you entertain a lot, purchase all-purpose wine glasses from a restaurant supply store—they typically come in cases of twenty-four and are very reasonably priced. The same goes for martini glasses if you serve a lot of cocktails at your parties. Or you may consider renting from a local party company. In addition to the fundamentals, these companies rent tables, large platters, martini glasses, and more. For table ornamentation, the simplest things can make a statement. Just head outdoors with a sturdy pair of shears and snip a few scented evergreen boughs or sprigs. Look around your house or check out garage or estate sales for unique pieces for serving or "décoring" your table. These need not be used as originally intended. For instance, little silver dishes can be filled with cranberries, then simple votives placed in the centers for a great holiday table. Or three or five (always an uneven number for aesthetic pleasure) laboratory beakers can be set down the center of your table, with a different type of green leaf or frond placed in each one. A gothic candelabra with slim tapers adorned with ornaments can be spectacular. I've done one with miniature white feathered birds that was stunning. The trick is contrast—mixing grand with delicate, harsh with frilly. For extra dramatic effect, however, I like to keep color schemes to one tone.

For napkins, pass on super-fussy folds and wine glass tucks. I like to tie oversized, crisply starched white napkins with a big knot, or fold them into a tidy, simple square set at each place. And place cards are a must for a well-laid dinner table. Remember, who sits next to whom can mean the difference between awkward silences and lively table talk. Pomegranates or shiny red apples personalized with a gold felt pen add a festive look.

My organizational method may be a bit more do-ahead work than you're used to, but it will give you a lot more time to spend with your guests. Since you have everything so "prepped," there'll be no need to get stressed out!

In the menus that follow, asterisked (*) items are suggestions of foods to purchase or pull from your own recipe files to accompany recipes from this book.

ROMANTIC DINNER

Perfect Ten 75

●

Butter Lettuce & Endive Salad with Avocado, Grapefruit & Pomegranate Seeds

●

New Century Lobster Américaine Poached in Herb Butter

●

Flaming Chocolate Cherry Alaska

Wine Suggestion

Chilled Champagne!

· · ·

FABULOUS FALL
DINNER FOR SIX

Gala Apple, Blue Cheese & Toasted Pecan Salad
with Cider Vinaigrette

·

Herb-Marinated Grilled Chicken Breasts

Wild Mushroom Risotto

Garlic & lemon sautéed kale or broccoli rape

*(Heat some olive oil in a very large pan, add some minced garlic,
and stir. Then add 2 bunches of washed and torn kale or broccoli
rape, sauté until tender, and season with salt and pepper and a
squeeze of lemon.)*

·

Free-Form Pear & Almond Tarts

Wine Suggestion

Syrah

• • •

POSH PATIO "PICNIC"

Herbed Crostini with assorted toppings

•

Crab Towers

•

Roasted Vegetable Risotto

•

Cherries Jubilee Parfaits

Wine Suggestions

With the crab, a dry riesling

With the risotto, a "juicy" merlot

• • •

REMEMBERING
SUNDAY DINNER

Wedge O'Lettuce with Blue Cheese & Beer Dressing

•

Sunday Slow-Cooked Roast Beef with Half a Bottle of Wine &
20 Cloves of Garlic

Confetti Garlic Mashed Potatoes

•

Hot chocolate chip cookies & frosty glasses of milk

Wine Suggestion

Zinfandel

NEW CLASSICS
COCKTAIL PARTY

Autumn Sidecar

Dubious Manhattan with Drunken Cherries

Terrific Classic 'Tini

Cosmo Chi Chi

•

Blue Cheese & Hazelnut–Stuffed Mushrooms

Thai Curry–Spiced Stuffed Eggs with Shrimp

Chipotle Deviled Eggs

Parmesan Poppy Seed Cheese Puffs

Sesame Cheddar Olive Poppers

Smoked Salmon with Wasabi Cream Cheese & Ginger Pickled Onions on Homemade Crackers

Sexy Baked Olives & Feta Cheese

What to do in advance

Thai Curry–Spiced and Chipotle Deviled Eggs Boil the eggs and peel them the day before. Stuff the eggs up to 6 hours before the party, cover, and refrigerate.

Parmesan Poppy Seed Cheese Puffs Make the batter up to 2 days in advance and refrigerate. Bake up to 8 hours in advance and reheat, or place on a baking sheet 1 day ahead, and cover and refrigerate until ready to bake.

Sexy Baked Olives & Feta Cheese Prepare in the pan up to 1 day in advance, cover, and refrigerate. Bring to room temperature and then bake right before serving.

Blue Cheese & Hazelnut–Stuffed Mushrooms Prepare, stuff, and arrange on a baking sheet up to 1 day in advance. Bake right before serving.

• • •

FIESTA WITH FRIENDS

Rosy 'Rita

•

Tropical Ceviche

Chili-Roasted Cashews

•

Wedge O'Lettuce with Green Goddess Dressing

•

Seared Steak with Chipotle Mushrooms & Crema

Cumin-Grilled Zucchini with Tomato-Corn Summer Salsa

Lemon-Spiked Basmati Rice

•

Frozen "Lemon Drop" Ice Topped with
a Lemon Cream Cloud

Wine Suggestion

A light Spanish red, such as Rioja, chilled—yes,
chilled—it's hot outside!

• • •

INEXPENSIVE
FANCY PANTS
"FAUX FRENCH"
DINNER

Baby Greens with Blackberry-Honey Vinaigrette,
Toasted Hazelnuts & Chèvre

•

Chardonnay Braised Chicken

Confetti Garlic Mashed Potatoes

•

Oozy Chocolate Grand Marnier Cakes with
Glazed Blood Oranges

Wine Suggestion

A good, cheap, red vin de pays or chardonnay

• • •

SURPRISE BREAKFAST
IN BED

Pan-Sized Berry Pancakes with Citrus Syrup

Crisp thick-sliced bacon

Steaming lattes

THE BIG
HOLIDAY FEAST

Hot Buttery Almond Rum

•

Seasonal Greens with Spicy Walnuts,
Crisp Asian Pears & Cranberry Vinaigrette

•

Roast Turkey with Old-Fashioned Turkey Mushroom Gravy

Ultimate Mom's Turkey Stuffing for a Crowd

Maple Scalloped Sweet Potatoes with Sage

Confetti Garlic Mashed Potatoes

Cranberry Pickled Pumpkin

Brussels Sprouts with Toasted Walnut Butter

•

Eggnog Bread Pudding with Rum Caramel

"Gimme Both" Pumpkin-Pecan Pie with Bourbon Whipped Cream

Wine Suggestions

A "juicy" merlot for the red wine drinkers

A cabernet franc rosé, or you can never go wrong with Champagne!

YOU LOVE TO ENTERTAIN BUT HATE ALL THE WORK. DO YOU KEEP SAY-
ING YOU'LL HAVE A LITTLE GET-TOGETHER BUT CAN NEVER GET IT
TOGETHER? WELL, HERE IS AN EFFORTLESS AND DELICIOUS DINNER
PARTY FOR EIGHT TO TEN PEOPLE THAT YOU CAN PUT TOGETHER IN
NO TIME AT ALL. IN FACT, IF YOU REALLY WANT TO MAKE IT EASY ON
YOURSELF, WHY NOT DIVVY UP THE TASKS WITH YOUR GUESTS? AND
NOT ONLY IS THIS MENU EASY, IT IS ALSO AFFORDABLE. SEE? NOW,
YOU CAN'T AFFORD NOT TO HAVE A PARTY! SO NO MORE EXCUSES—
GET COOKING WITH YOUR FRIENDS! HERE'S THE BREAKDOWN OF THE
DINNER, COMPLETE WITH A SUGGESTED DELEGATION OF DUTIES:

● ● ●

"SHARE THE WORK"
SUMMER ENTERTAINING

Guest Prosciutto-Wrapped Melon with White Balsamic & Honey
Mint Drizzle

Guest *(Host supplies the grill)* Grilled Bread with Bruschetta
Tomatoes

Host or Guest *Assorted high-quality olives*

●

Guest Shaved Fennel & Arugula Salad with Lemon Vinaigrette

●

Host Chicken, Artichoke & Parmesan Baked Penne

●

Host Fresh Berries with Fluffy Vin Santo Zabaglione &
Hazelnut Biscotti

Wine Suggestion

Chianti or cabernet franc

SIMPLE SUMMER
SUPPER

Mahali's Sky

•

Best of the Season Gazpacho

•

Crab Soufflé Cakes with Sweet Pepper & Corn Relish

•

Succulent Summer Stone Fruits with Lavender-Infused Honey Syrup

Vanilla bean ice cream

Wine Suggestion

Pinot gris

• • •

TIKI TORCH DREAMIN'

Ginger Jasmine Lime Rickey

•

Warm Spinach Salad with Shiitake Mushrooms,
Sweet Peppers & Sesame Honey Dressing

•

Roasted Shrimp with Thai Lime Butter

Colorful Jasmine Rice

Sautéed sugar peas

•

Tropical Fruit Shortcake with Coconut Cream

Wine Suggestion

Fumé blanc

• • •

AUTUMN FIRESIDE
DINNER

Roasted Pork Loin with Fennel Spice Rub

Sweet & Sour Ruby Cabbage

Steamed fingerling potatoes or roasted red potatoes

•

Unbelievable Apple Cake with Cider Crème Anglaise
& Cranberry Compote

Wine Suggestion

A big, "chewy" cabernet

· · ·

General Recipe Notes

- Butter is salted unless otherwise noted.

- Flour is all-purpose unless otherwise noted.

- Ginger is peeled unless otherwise noted.

- Onions and carrots are peeled unless otherwise noted.

- **To make lemon or other citrus zest** Lemon zest is made from the outer peel of the fruit—with no white pith remaining. You can use a fine zesting tool that makes long, very thin, pretty strands, or you can peel off the zest with an ordinary potato peeler, being sure not to get any white pith, and then finely cut it in very, very thin, long strips or mince it.

- **To make chipotle pepper purée** Place the contents of 1 can of chipotle peppers in adobo sauce (found in the Mexican foods section of well-stocked grocers) in a blender or food processor and purée until smooth. Freeze any remaining purée for another use, such as spicing up ketchup or barbecue sauce.

- **To toast hazelnuts** Place the hazelnuts on a baking sheet and toast in preheated 350°F oven for about 6 to 8 minutes, or until golden. When cool enough to handle, put the hazelnuts in a clean, non-fuzzy dishtowel and rub as much skin off the hazelnuts as will come off easily.

- Raw eggs, raw fish, and raw shellfish are not recommended for pregnant women, children, the elderly, or anyone with immune deficiencies.

- Cooking is an art, not a science. Ovens and burner strengths vary, as do different ingredients in different parts of the country. Use your best judgment when making the recipes in this book.

SIPS

Homemade Sweet & Sour

Perfect Ten 75

Rosy 'Rita

Cosmo Chi Chi

Rosemary Rhubarb Meyer Lemonade

Melon Mélange

Winter Spiced White Wine

Terrific Classic 'Tini

Dubious Manhattan with Drunken Cherries

Autumn Sidecar

Juicy Strawberry Pineapple Sangría

Ginger Jasmine Lime Rickey

Mahali's Sky

Sake Punch

Coconutty Adult Mocha

Hot Buttery Almond Rum

Makes 2 cups

THIS COCKTAIL MIX IS THE REAL THING. YOU'LL BE AMAZED AT THE DIFFERENCE IT WILL MAKE. HOMEMADE SWEET & SOUR IS REALLY FRESH TASTING, A WORLD APART FROM BOTTLED PRODUCTS. THIS ONE INGREDIENT ALONE CAN TAKE YOUR COCKTAILS TO THE PINNACLE OF SUCCESS.

• • •

HOMEMADE SWEET & SOUR

½ cup fresh lime juice

½ cup fresh lemon juice

1 cup Simple Syrup (recipe follows)

In a large jar with a lid, combine all ingredients. Cover and keep refrigerated for up to 2 weeks, or freeze.

For a Fresh Lime or Lemon Sour variation: Use all fresh lime juice or all fresh lemon juice.

Makes 7 cups

• • •

SIMPLE SYRUP

4 cups sugar

4 cups water

Combine sugar and water in a heavy pan. Bring to a boil, stirring to dissolve the sugar. Boil for 2 minutes. Remove from the heat and let cool. Bottle and store at room temperature until needed. It keeps indefinitely.

CHEF'S TIPS:
You can make up a large batch of Homemade Sweet & Sour, then divide the mix among several freezer containers. That way you'll always have some ready to defrost and use.

TURN A CLASSIC DRINK INTO A PERFECT "TEN." THIS TAKE ON THE SOPHISTICATED FRENCH 75 COCKTAIL SINGS WITH THE BOTANICAL ESSENCES OF TANQUERAY TEN GIN.

• • •

PERFECT TEN 75

1½ ounces (3 tablespoons) Tanqueray TEN gin

½ ounce (1 tablespoon) Grand Marnier

1 ounce (2 tablespoons) Fresh Lemon Sour (page 28)

2 to 3 ounces (4 to 6 tablespoons) chilled brut Champagne

Long orange peel twist for garnish

Fill a cocktail shaker with ice and add the gin, Grand Marnier, and Fresh Lemon Sour. Shake until very cold, at least 10 times. Strain the drink into a large martini glass, and top with the Champagne. Garnish with a curled twist of orange peel hanging over the edge of the glass. When zesting the orange twist, work over the drink so the flavorful oils spritz into the cocktail.

Makes 1 cocktail

SALT ON THE RIM OF MARGARITA GLASSES IS A TRADITION, BUT I LIKE TO LEAVE THE RIM ON THIS DRINK NAKED WHEN ADDING FRUITY ALIZÉ RED PASSION, COGNAC BLENDED WITH PASSION FRUIT AND CRANBERRY. IT SINKS TO THE BOTTOM, CREATING A COOL, TWO-TONED, LAYERED LOOK.

• • •

ROSY 'RITA

1 small lime wedge (⅛ lime)

1½ ounces (3 tablespoons) high-quality tequila

1 ounce (2 tablespoons) Fresh Lime Sour (page 28)

½ ounce (1 tablespoon) Alizé Red Passion

Squeeze the lime wedge into a cocktail shaker, then drop in the wedge. Fill with ice, then add the tequila and Fresh Lime Sour.

Cap and shake well, then strain into a large martini glass. Slowly drizzle the Alizé Red Passion into the drink.

Makes 1 cocktail

I CREATED THIS PERKY PINK COCKTAIL FOR THE SUSAN G. KOMEN BREAST CANCER FOUNDATION GALA IN 2000. IT WAS THE HIT OF THE EVENING!

• • •

COSMO CHI CHI

1½ ounces (3 tablespoons) high-quality vodka

¼ ounce (1½ teaspoons) Grand Marnier

¾ ounce (1½ tablespoons) cranberry juice

1½ ounces (3 tablespoons) Tropical Sweet & Sour (recipe follows)

1 frozen whole cranberry for garnish

Fill a cocktail shaker with ice and add all ingredients. Cap and shake until very cold—at least 10 times. Strain the drink into an oversized martini glass. Float a whole cranberry on top.

Makes about 2 cups, or enough for 10 cocktails

• • •

TROPICAL SWEET & SOUR

½ cup Simple Syrup (page 28)

¼ cup fresh lime juice

¼ cup fresh lemon juice

¾ cup pineapple juice

3 tablespoons Coco Lopez (sweetened cream of coconut)

In a decorative bottle (because it looks nice when serving), shake all of the ingredients together. Refrigerate until ready to use. Shake well before each use. The mix can be stored, refrigerated, for up to 2 weeks.

THIS RECIPE TAKES A BIT OF WORK TO MAKE BUT IS WORTH EVERY MINUTE. IF YOU ARE REALLY AMBITIOUS, YOU CAN MAKE A FEW BATCHES AND FREEZE SOME FOR GRAYER DAYS. I LIKE TO SERVE THIS FOR ALL KINDS OF OCCASIONS (SEE THE CHEF'S TIPS). THE MEYER LEMON IS A BACKYARD FRUIT IN BOTH CALIFORNIA AND FLORIDA. THIS HIGHLY AROMATIC FRUIT, SWEETER THAN STANDARD LEMONS, IS BEGIN-NING TO BE SEEN IN GROCERY STORES, BUT ITS SHELF LIFE IS LIMITED. WATCH CLOSELY FOR IT IN THE WINTER MONTHS, OR ASK YOUR FRIENDS VISITING THOSE AREAS TO BRING YOU SOME BACK . . . THEY ARE WELL WORTH THE SCHLEP.

• • •

ROSEMARY RHUBARB MEYER LEMONADE

2 large Meyer lemons (or substitute regular lemons)

1 cup high-quality honey

4 cups water

4 cups diced fresh rhubarb

2 teaspoons minced fresh rosemary

Fresh rosemary sprigs for garnish

With a potato peeler, remove only the yellow skin of the lemons. With a sharp knife, slice this zest into fine strips.

Cut the lemons in half and squeeze the juice into a 4-cup or 8-cup measure. Do not strain the juice—you want to keep all the pulp—just pick out any seeds. Add the lemon zest strips, cover, and refrigerate.

CHEF'S TIPS:

● *If you're serving this nonalcoholic drink at a more elegant affair, shake the lemonade in your trusty cocktail shaker with lots of ice, strain into oversized martini glasses, and drop in a tiny sprig of rosemary for garnish.*

● *This 'ade's also fabulous as a gin or vodka libation. Add 1 shot of gin or vodka per serving.*

● *For a fun brunch drink, offer this lemonade chilled over ice in champagne glasses and top it off with a splash of bubbly or club soda. For patio refreshment, serve it on the rocks in tall glasses.*

Meanwhile, place the honey, water, rhubarb, and minced rosemary in a saucepan over medium-high heat. Bring to a slow simmer and cook, uncovered, for 4 to 5 minutes, until the rhubarb is tender. Remove from the heat and let sit at room temperature until cool. Strain through a fine-mesh strainer, letting the juice drip through. To keep the juice clear, do not press on the mixture in the strainer. (You can let it strain overnight, refrigerated, if you wish.)

Add the strained juice to the measuring cup containing the lemon juice and zest. Stir and add water to make 6 cups total. Pour into a decorative pitcher.

For each serving, pour about 6 ounces (¾ cup) over ice in a tall glass, with a sprig of rosemary for garnish.

Makes 2 drinks

BE SURE TO USE A SUPER-RIPE AND JUICY HONEYDEW MELON IN THIS RECIPE.

• • •

MELON MÉLANGE

1½ cups cracked ice

½ ounce (1 tablespoon) fresh lime juice

1 cup diced ripe honeydew melon

2 ounces (¼ cup) melon liqueur

2 ounces (¼ cup) vodka

2 ounces (¼ cup) orange juice

Place all of the drink ingredients in a blender and blend until smooth and no ice chunks remain. Pour into large, chilled balloon wine glasses or tumblers. Garnish with mint or melon ball skewers and serve.

For a spicy variation: Add ½ teaspoon minced ginger to the blender.

GARNISHES

Large sprigs of mint

Skewers of melon balls

CHEF'S TIPS:

• *Especially fun garnishes are skewers alternating different kinds and colors of melons—cantaloupe, Persian, Crenshaw, honeydew, and red and yellow watermelon.*

• *Accompany this drink with a fresh fruit salsa of chopped pineapple, watermelon, and sliced green grapes. Add a sprinkle of salt, some chopped fresh cilantro, a splash of lime juice, and some chopped jalapeño for kick. Serve on the sunny patio with tortilla chips for dipping!*

Makes 7 cups, or about 8 servings

FOR A BIG SOCIAL CELEBRATION, WHY NOT BREW UP A BATCH OF WINTER SPICED WHITE WINE INSTEAD OF THE SAME-OLD-SAME-OLD SPICED CIDER? THIS STEAMY WHITE-WINE INFUSION IS FLAVORED WITH PEARS, APPLES, ORANGES, CLOVES, ALLSPICE, AND CINNAMON AND SLIGHTLY SWEETENED WITH BROWN SUGAR. WITH A LITTLE GRAND MARNIER FOR A PUNCH, IT IS SURE TO BE A HIT.

• • •

WINTER SPICED WHITE WINE

**2 (750 ml) bottles
light, dry white wine,
such as chenin blanc**

**1 pear, cut crosswise
into ¼-inch slices**

**1 apple, cut crosswise
into ¼-inch slices**

**1 orange, poked with
12 whole cloves, then cut
into ¼-inch slices**

5 allspice berries

**1 cinnamon stick,
broken in half**

⅓ cup packed brown sugar

**4 ounces (½ cup)
Grand Marnier**

**Orange peel twists
for garnish**

Place all the ingredients in a stainless steel or flameproof glass pan and stir well to incorporate the brown sugar. Place over low heat and warm. Do not boil! Let the flavors steep for at least 30 minutes before serving.

At this point you can keep the wine warm and serve, or chill it for later. To reheat, warm each portion in a microwave until just hot but not boiling. Garnish each serving with a twist of orange peel.

CHEF'S TIPS:

● *For large parties, this recipe can easily be increased,
made in advance, and then gently reheated before serving.*

● *Keep large batches warm in a crockpot on low
heat or in a deep, pretty chafing dish.*

● *For a beautiful presentation, garnish with orange
peel twists made with a channel knife—available
at specialty kitchen shops.*

Makes 1 cocktail　　THE KEY TO A DIVINE MARTINI IS TO BE SURE EVERYTHING IS WELL
CHILLED. USE LOTS OF ICE TO CHILL YOUR GLASS AND WHEN SHAKING
YOUR MARTINI.

• • •

TERRIFIC CLASSIC 'TINI

**⅛ ounce (¾ teaspoon)
dry vermouth**

**1½ ounces (3 tablespoons)
high-quality vodka
or high-quality gin**

**Stuffed olive or lemon
peel twist for garnish**

Fill a small martini glass with ice and a splash of water to chill.
Meanwhile, splash the vermouth into a cocktail shaker, swirl, and
shake out the vermouth. Fill the shaker to the top with ice. Add the
vodka or gin. Shake until very cold—at least 15 times. Empty the ice
from the martini glass. Strain the drink into the martini glass. Skewer
an olive on a toothpick and drop it into the drink, or garnish the drink
with a lemon twist.

CHEF'S TIPS:

*For my gatherings, I love to take pitted, unstuffed green
olives and stuff them with different yummies, such as blue cheese or
toasted whole almonds. Or, thread my lemon twists through the olives,
and let guests garnish their own 'tini with their favorite.*

Makes 1 cocktail

FRENCH DUBONNET ROUGE, AN APÉRITIF WINE, GIVES THIS CLASSIC COCKTAIL TYPICALLY MADE WITH RED VERMOUTH A LESS-SWEET TWIST.

• • •

DUBIOUS MANHATTAN
WITH DRUNKEN CHERRIES

¾ ounce (1½ tablespoons) Dubonnet rouge

1½ ounces (3 tablespoons) bourbon

3 Drunken Cherries (recipe follows) for garnish

Fill a cocktail shaker with ice. Measure in the Dubonnet and bourbon. Cap the shaker and shake until cold—at least 10 times.

Strain into a martini glass. Skewer the Drunken Cherries onto a cocktail pick and drop it into the drink.

Makes 1 cup

• • •

DRUNKEN CHERRIES

½ cup dried sweet cherries

½ cup Dubonnet rouge

¼ cup sugar

¼ cup hot water

Place the cherries, Dubonnet, and sugar in a small bowl. Pour the hot water over the cherries and stir well. Cover and let sit at room temperature for at least 12 hours before using. Store, covered and refrigerated, for up to 2 months.

CHEF'S TIPS:
• Plumped dried cherries are a great
alternative to maraschino cherries.
• Try making the recipe with dried tart cherries instead.
If you want to keep the flavor of the cherries more neutral for use
in other drinks, substitute ¼ cup vodka for the Dubonnet,
and increase the sugar and water to ½ cup each.

Makes 1 cocktail

AN OLD CLASSIC MAKES ITS WAY BACK TO THE HIP COCKTAIL SCENE. THIS TIME, IT GETS A NEW FLAIR WITH THE ADDITION OF HAZELNUT-FLAVORED FRANGELICO AND TUACA'S UNIQUE BLEND OF BRANDY, VANILLA, AND CITRUS ESSENCES.

• • •

AUTUMN SIDECAR

¼ of an orange or ½ of a small tangerine

1½ ounces (3 tablespoons) Homemade Sweet & Sour (page 28)

1 ounce (2 tablespoons) brandy or cognac

½ ounce (1 tablespoon) Tuaca

½ ounce (1 tablespoon) Frangelico

GARNISHES

Superfine sugar for rimming glass (optional)

1 toasted hazelnut (page 25)

If you want to rim your glass with sugar, first wipe the edge of a martini glass all around with a piece of orange, then dip it into superfine sugar.

Squeeze the orange or tangerine into a cocktail shaker and drop it in. Fill with ice and add the Homemade Sweet & Sour, brandy, Tuaca, and Frangelico. Cap the shaker and shake vigorously—at least 10 times. Strain into a martini glass and float a toasted hazelnut on top.

CHEF'S TIPS:
When storing toasted hazelnuts, do not refrigerate, as this will make them soft.

Makes 6 cups, or about 8 servings

TRADITIONALLY, SANGRÍA IS MADE WITH RED WINE, FRUITS, AND A BIT OF SOME KIND OF SPIRIT, SUCH AS BRANDY. BUT WHO SAYS YOU HAVE TO FOLLOW THE RULES? I CERTAINLY NEVER DO! THE ADD-INS, AS WELL AS THE KINDS OF WINE YOU CAN USE, ARE UNLIMITED—FROM WHITE SANGRÍA TO VERSIONS WITH GINGER ALE TO TROPICAL ONES WITH MANGOES OR PASSION FRUIT AND CHAMPAGNE. WITH PINEAPPLES, STRAWBERRIES, AND A SUN-DRENCHED WINE, THIS SANGRÍA ADDS UP TO A VERY TASTEFUL CARMEN MIRANDA OF VINOUS DELIGHTS.

JUICY STRAWBERRY PINEAPPLE SANGRÍA

1 (750 ml) bottle red wine

1 lemon, thinly sliced

1 cup thinly sliced fresh strawberries

1 cup diced fresh pineapple

2 ounces (¼ cup) cassis, Chambord, or other berry liqueur

¼ cup packed brown sugar

Pineapple leaves for garnish

In a pitcher, combine all ingredients and stir with a spoon, crushing some of the berries. (I like to stick my clean fingers in and squish some of the berries by hand!) Refrigerate to let the flavors marry for at least 2 hours before serving.

Serve over ice, garnished with pineapple leaves.

CHEF'S TIPS:

- *Garnish your drinks with the pineapple leaves, letting them stick up out of the glasses.*
- *Try making this with a "juicy" red wine such as a French Côtes du Rhone or a Spanish tinto.*

Makes 1 drink

THIS REFRESHING NONALCOHOLIC SPRITZER IS LIKE A PERFECT SUNNY DAY. IF YOU PREFER, ADD VODKA OR GIN.

• • •

GINGER JASMINE LIME RICKEY

2 ounces (¼ cup) Lime Syrup (recipe follows)

4 ounces (½ cup) sparkling water or club soda

Lime wedge or curl of lime peel for garnish

Fill a large glass with ice. Add the Lime Syrup, then splash in the sparkling water or club soda. Stir and serve immediately. Garnish with a fresh lime wedge or a curled lime twist.

Makes enough for 6 drinks

• • •

LIME SYRUP

1 tablespoon minced ginger

1 cup fresh lime juice

¾ cup sugar

½ cup water

2 tablespoons loose jasmine tea

In a small, heavy saucepan, combine the ginger, lime juice, sugar, and water. Bring to a boil over high heat and boil for 2 minutes. Remove from the heat and stir in the tea. Steep for 5 minutes, then strain through a very fine strainer, pressing out as much liquid as possible. Discard the solids. Refrigerate the syrup until ready to use. Store, refrigerated, for up to 7 days.

CHEF'S TIPS:
For a fun and creative way to serve this drink, use fresh lemongrass as a "stir stick."

Makes 1 cocktail

I CREATED THIS SIGNATURE COCKTAIL FOR WOODLAND PARK ZOO. INSPIRED BY A 12-YEAR-OLD GIRAFFE NAMED MAHALI, I IMAGINED THAT THIS DRINK'S BEAUTIFUL BLUE COLOR MUST BE WHAT THE SKY LOOKS LIKE . . . WAY UP THERE.

• • •

MAHALI'S SKY

2 large sprigs fresh mint

¼ ounce (1½ teaspoons) blue curaçao

2 ounces (¼ cup) Bacardi Limon rum

½ ounce (1 tablespoon) Malibu coconut rum

1½ ounces (3 tablespoons) Fresh Lime Sour (page 28)

2 ounces (¼ cup) club soda

Crush the mint and drop it into a cocktail shaker. Fill to the top with ice. Add the blue curaçao and the Bacardi Limon rum. Add the Malibu rum and the Fresh Lime Sour. Top with the club soda.

Cap the shaker and shake vigorously. Do not strain. Pour into a large, tall glass.

CHEF'S TIPS:

When creating and serving innovative cocktails, be sure to garnish them only with things that are a part of the drink. For instance, I would garnish this drink only with a fresh sprig of mint. Pleeeease . . . no cherry orange skewers. However, umbrellas are approved!

Makes 5 cups, or about
6 servings

THIS REFRESHING SANGRÍA-STYLE PUNCH COMBINES AN ATYPICAL MIXTURE OF SAKE AND ZESTY CITRUS FRUITS WITH THE ENERGIZING ZING OF GINGER AND LEMONGRASS.

● ● ●

SAKE PUNCH

1 (750 ml) bottle sake

6 tablespoons honey

2-inch piece of ginger, peeled and thinly sliced

1 stalk fresh lemongrass, split in half lengthwise, then cut in 3- to 4-inch pieces

1 lemon, thinly sliced

1 large tangerine or orange, thinly sliced

1 large black or red plum, pitted and thinly sliced into wedges (substitute apricots or any other stone fruit if plums are not available)

In a pitcher, combine all ingredients and stir with a spoon, crushing some of the fruit. Refrigerate overnight, or for at least 12 hours, to let the flavors marry before serving. Use within 4 days of making.

Serve over ice, including some of the fruit in each serving.

CHEF'S TIPS:

In crafting this punch, I tried several different brands of sake and found that an inexpensive dry sake definitely works. For truly sublime refreshment, however, try the recipe at least once with a premium junmai sake. I use Momokawa Silver Sake, which is fragrant with notes of pears, citrus, and even a hint of watermelon rind. Kampai!

WHEN THE WEATHER TURNS NIPPY, NOTHING DISPELS A CHILL BETTER THAN A STEAMING HOT CUP OF COFFEE LACED WITH A DELICIOUS, DECADENT LIQUEUR. IT WARMS YOUR HANDS AND HEATS UP YOUR PSYCHE AS WELL.

• • •

COCONUTTY ADULT MOCHA

½ ounce (1 tablespoon) Malibu rum

1 ounce (2 tablespoons) dark rum

1 ounce (2 tablespoons) dark chocolate sauce

5 to 6 ounces (about ¾ cup) hot premium coffee

GARNISHES

Dark chocolate sauce and shredded coconut for rimming glass

Whipped cream or Coconut Cream (page 173)

To rim the cup with coconut: Dip the rim of a mug or glass coffee cup into some chocolate sauce, then press it into the coconut.

To make the drink: Measure both rums and then the chocolate sauce directly into the mug or glass cup. Stir in the coffee.

Dollop with a pouf of whipped cream or Coconut Cream and serve.

CHEF'S TIPS:
Be sure your coffee is really hot when making coffee drinks with lots of other ingredients—otherwise your drink will not be warm enough.

FOR A WHIMSICAL PRESENTATION, DECORATE YOUR MUGS AHEAD OF TIME BY DIPPING THE RIMS INTO WHITE CHOCOLATE OR CARAMEL SAUCE. THEN PRESS THE RIMS INTO FINELY CHOPPED ALMONDS FOR AN ALMOND-CRUSTED RIM.

• • •

HOT BUTTERY ALMOND RUM

3 tablespoons Almond Butter Batter (recipe follows)

1 ounce (2 tablespoons) dark or spiced rum

5 ounces (½ cup plus 2 tablespoons) boiling water

Place the Almond Butter Batter and rum in a coffee glass or mug. Add the boiling water and stir until the batter is dissolved. Serve.

Makes about 5 cups, or enough for about 24 drinks

• • •

ALMOND BUTTER BATTER

½ pound (2 sticks) butter, softened

6 ounces marzipan (almond paste)

1½ cups packed light brown sugar

1¾ cups powdered sugar

1 pint high-quality vanilla ice cream, softened

1 tablespoon vanilla extract

1½ teaspoons almond extract

1½ teaspoons ground cinnamon

1½ teaspoons ground nutmeg

With an electric mixer or a wooden spoon, cream the butter, marzipan, and sugars together in a mixing bowl until the ingredients are thoroughly combined and slightly fluffy. Mix in the remaining ingredients until thoroughly combined. Store, refrigerated, for up to 1 week, or freeze for up to 1 month.

• • •

TEASERS

Chipotle Deviled Eggs

Thai Curry–Spiced Stuffed Eggs with Shrimp

Grilled Bread with Bruschetta Tomatoes

Warm Almond-Crusted Brie with
Apple-Onion Compote

Prosciutto-Wrapped Melon with White
Balsamic & Honey Mint Drizzle

Chili-Roasted Cashews

Steamed Mussels in Thai Basil Coconut Broth

Parmesan Poppy Seed Cheese Puffs

Crab Towers

Sesame Cheddar Olive Poppers

Smoked Salmon with Wasabi Cream Cheese
& Ginger Pickled Onions on Homemade Crackers

Herbed Crostini

Sexy Baked Olives & Feta Cheese

Blue Cheese & Hazelnut–Stuffed Mushrooms

Tropical Ceviche

WHEN I STARTED MAKING DEVILED EGGS AND BRINGING THEM TO PAR-
TIES IN THE EARLY NINETIES, I DID IT ALMOST AS A JOKE. REEEEALLY—A
CHEF BRINGING DEVILED EGGS TO A PARTY—CAN YOU IMAGINE? WELL,
I WAS SICK OF ALWAYS HAVING TO MAKE SOMETHING "SPECTACULAR"!
WOULDN'T YOU KNOW IT—THIS SPICY TWIST ON AN OLD FAVORITE
BECAME A HUGE HIT AND MUST BE AMONG MY MOST REQUESTED
RECIPES EVER.

• • •

CHIPOTLE DEVILED EGGS

1 dozen large eggs

**3 tablespoons regular or
low-fat sour cream**

3 tablespoons mayonnaise

½ teaspoon salt

**½ teaspoon Dijon
mustard, optional**

**1 to 2 tablespoons chipotle
pepper purée (page 25)**

1 teaspoon minced garlic

**2 tablespoons very thinly
sliced green onion**

TOPPING

**½ cup diced
(¼-inch) tomatoes**

**1 tablespoon
minced white onion**

**2 tablespoons minced
fresh cilantro**

**1 to 2 teaspoons chipotle
pepper purée (page 25)**

Place the eggs in a saucepan and cover with cool water to 1 inch
above the eggs. Bring to a boil over medium-high heat, then time 10
minutes. After eggs have cooked for 10 minutes, remove from the
heat and run cool water over them. When they are cool, carefully
peel under running water.

Cut the eggs in half lengthwise and remove the yolks to a mixing
bowl. Set the egg white halves on a platter, cover, and refrigerate.

Mash the egg yolks to a smooth consistency with a fork or potato
masher. Mix in the sour cream, mayonnaise, salt, mustard, 1 to 2 tablespoons chipotle purée, and garlic until smooth. (You can also do this
in a mixing bowl with a whip attachment.) Stir in the green onions.
Spoon the yolk mixture into a pastry bag fitted with a plain or large
star tip and then squeeze (pipe) the mixture evenly into the egg white
halves.

To make the topping: In a small bowl, mix together tomatoes, onion,
cilantro, and chipotle purée. Top each egg half with 1 teaspoon of
the tomato mixture.

THAI YELLOW CURRY PASTE IS AVAILABLE AT WELL-STOCKED
GROCERS AND ASIAN MARKETS.

• • •

THAI CURRY–SPICED STUFFED EGGS WITH SHRIMP

1 dozen large eggs

2 teaspoons Thai yellow curry paste

1 teaspoon minced garlic

1 teaspoon minced ginger

2 teaspoons Dijon mustard

¼ teaspoon Tabasco

½ cup mayonnaise

4 ounces bay shrimp, well-drained and chopped

1 tablespoon chopped fresh cilantro

1 tablespoon chopped fresh mint

To cook the eggs: Follow procedure in Chipotle Deviled Eggs, above.

Place the yolks and curry paste in a mixing bowl and whip until smooth. (If you don't have a mixer, mash the yolks to a smooth consistency with a fork or potato masher.) Add the garlic, ginger, Dijon mustard, Tabasco, and mayonnaise, and mix until smooth. Mix in HALF of the chopped shrimp.

Note: Most Thai curry pastes are very salty, so no additional salt is added to the recipe. However, be sure to taste the yolk mixture; if more salt is needed, carefully add it to taste.

Spoon the yolk mixture into a pastry bag fitted with a plain or large star tip and then squeeze (pipe) the mixture evenly into the egg white halves. (Or spoon the mixture into the egg white halves.)

In a small bowl, mix together the remaining chopped shrimp, cilantro, and mint. Top each egg half with a bit of the mixture, dividing it evenly among the eggs.

CHEF'S TIPS:

*Get yourself a few of those great new "disposable" plastic
piping bags and a nice big star tip. These bags make it so much easier to
squeeze fillings than always having to wash out a canvas piping bag.
If you are in a pinch for a piping bag, use a plastic sandwich bag
with a small part of the corner cut off.*

WHILE GUESTS ARE GATHERING FOR YOUR OUTDOOR PARTY, HAVE SLICES OF TOASTY RUSTIC BREAD JUST COMING OFF THE GRILL. TOP EACH WITH A BIG SPOONFUL OF BRUSCHETTA TOMATOES—A FLAVOR-FUL TOSSING OF RIPE TOMATOES, FRESH BASIL, ONIONS, GARLIC, AND SALT—AND OFFER THEM TO NEW ARRIVALS.

• • •

GRILLED BREAD WITH BRUSCHETTA TOMATOES

3 tablespoons extra virgin olive oil

3 cups chopped vine-ripe tomatoes (2 to 3 medium tomatoes)

¼ cup chopped fresh basil

2 tablespoons minced red onion

1½ teaspoons minced garlic

¾ teaspoon kosher salt

1 loaf rustic artisan bread or baguette

Freshly ground black pepper

Preheat the grill to a medium-high heat.

In a medium bowl, toss together 2 tablespoons of the olive oil, tomatoes, basil, onion, garlic, and salt, and set aside.

If using a large, "fat" loaf, cut it with a serrated knife into six ½-inch slices, then slice each piece in half crosswise, making 12 pieces. If using a baguette-style loaf, cut twelve ½-inch slices from the loaf. (Serve any remaining bread with dinner.) Brush both sides of the bread with the remaining 1 tablespoon olive oil and grill on each side until lightly marked or toasted.

Place on a platter and immediately top with the reserved tomato mixture. Sprinkle with freshly ground black pepper.

CHEF'S TIPS:
When colorful heirloom tomatoes are in season and at their summer peak, try a fun combination of green Mister Stripey, Cherokee Purple, and orange Earl of Edgecomb.

PREPARE THE BRIE WEDGES AT LEAST 4 HOURS IN ADVANCE SO THE ALMOND BREADING SETS WELL. YOU CAN MAKE THE COMPOTE UP TO 3 DAYS IN ADVANCE AND BRING IT TO ROOM TEMPERATURE BEFORE SERVING. BESIDES SERVING THIS AS AN APPETIZER, I LIKE TO OFFER IT AS AN AFTER-DINNER CHEESE COURSE.

• • •

WARM ALMOND-CRUSTED BRIE WITH APPLE-ONION COMPOTE

About ¼ cup flour

1 egg

1 tablespoon water

1 cup (3 to 4 ounces) sliced almonds, with skin, very finely chopped

1 (8-ounce) wheel Brie, cut into 6 wedges

Thinly sliced French bread

Apple-Onion Compote (recipe follows)

Granny Smith or other green apples, cut into wedges, optional

Place the flour in a small bowl. In another small bowl, whisk together the egg and water. Place the chopped almonds in a flat dish.

Dust the Brie wedges in the flour, dip them in the egg wash, then coat them well with almonds, pressing them in to completely coat the cheese. Place the prepared cheese wedges, 2 inches apart, on a baking sheet, cover with plastic wrap, and chill thoroughly for at least 4 hours before serving time.

Preheat the oven to 425°F. Bake the Brie until the crust is golden and the interior is just hot all the way through but not oozing out, 4 to 5 minutes. Serve immediately, with French bread, Apple-Onion Compote, and apple slices if desired.

APPLE-ONION COMPOTE

1 large green apple, cored and cut into chunks

¼ small white onion, cut into chunks

1 tablespoon butter

½ teaspoon very finely minced ginger

¼ teaspoon minced lemon zest

1½ teaspoons cider vinegar

⅓ cup red pepper jam

1 tablespoon dried currants (or substitute chopped raisins)

In a food processor, pulse the apple and onion until they are chopped into ¼- to ⅓-inch pieces.

In a medium skillet, melt the butter over medium-high heat. Add the apple, onion, and ginger. Sauté for about 5 minutes, or until the apple and onion are just tender.

Add the lemon zest, vinegar, pepper jam, and currants, and bring to a boil. Let the mixture boil for about 2 minutes, until loose and chutneylike. Remove from the heat and cool.

CHEF'S TIPS:
How to bread items—without breading your fingers!
Use one hand as your "wet" hand and the other as your "dry" hand.
It takes a bit of practice to avoid getting them mixed up, but soon
you will master this chef's technique.

Makes 8 to 10 servings

THIS DELICIOUS APPETIZER IS PERFECT WHEN SERVED AT A SUMMER GATHERING AS PART OF A BUFFET, GROANING-BOARD STYLE. A SIMPLE COMBINATION OF WHITE BALSAMIC VINEGAR, MIXED WITH A SMIDGEN OF HONEY AND MINCED FRESH MINT, THEN DRIZZLED OVER A BIG PLATTER OF SUCCULENT CANTALOUPE WEDGES WRAPPED WITH SHAVED PROSCIUTTO, MAKES AN IMPRESSIVE "FANCY PANTS" STARTER COURSE. OFFER MORE OF THE SAUCE ALONGSIDE FOR DRIZZLING.

● ● ●

PROSCIUTTO-WRAPPED MELON WITH WHITE BALSAMIC & HONEY MINT DRIZZLE

1 small, ripe cantaloupe

⅓ pound prosciutto, or 8 to 10 paper-thin slices

¼ cup white balsamic vinegar

2 tablespoons high-quality honey

1 tablespoon finely chopped fresh mint

Lay the cantaloupe on its side and, with a serrated knife, cut 1 inch from each end. Turn the cantaloupe on one end and, following the circumference of the melon, cut off the skin just down to the melon flesh, being sure no green remains. Cut the melon in half, lengthwise, and scoop out the seeds and membrane. Cut the melon into 8 to 10 wedges, place on a platter, and drape each wedge with a piece of prosciutto.

To make the White Balsamic & Honey Mint Drizzle: Mix together vinegar, honey, and mint in a cup or small bowl. When ready to serve, drizzle some of the mixture over the prosciutto-draped melon, and offer the remainder alongside.

CHEF'S TIPS:
● *Choose melons that are summer sun–ripened. Smell the melon—if it smells good and "melony," then it probably tastes the same.*
● *Have your grocer slice the prosciutto paper-thin for you.*

NOTHING DISAPPEARS AT A PARTY FASTER THAN THESE SALTY, SAVORY, AND SLIGHTLY SPICY NUTS!

• • •

CHILI-ROASTED CASHEWS

1 egg white

1 tablespoon water

1 pound (about 3½ cups) salted, roasted cashews

⅓ cup sugar

1 tablespoon mild chili powder

2 teaspoons ground cumin

2 teaspoons kosher salt

½ teaspoon cayenne

Preheat the oven to 250°F.

In a medium bowl, whisk the egg white with the water until foamy. Add the cashews and toss to coat. Transfer the nuts to a strainer, shake, and let drain for at least 2 minutes.

In a large bowl, mix together the sugar, chili powder, cumin, salt, and cayenne. Add the nuts and toss to coat thoroughly.

On a large, rimmed baking sheet, spread the nuts out in a single layer. Bake for 40 minutes. Stir the nuts with a spatula and spread them out again. REDUCE THE TEMPERATURE to 200°F and bake for 30 minutes longer, until the nuts are dry.

Using a spatula, loosen the nuts on the baking sheet, but do not remove them from the sheet. Cool to room temperature. Be sure to let the nuts cool completely and become crisp. Store in an airtight container at room temperature for up to 2 weeks.

CHEF'S TIPS:

● *This basic recipe can be used with whole almonds or unsalted, skinless peanuts instead of the cashews.*
● *If the nuts lose their crispness after cooking, toast them in a 350°F oven for a couple of minutes before serving.*
● *When using different-sized varieties of nuts, you may need to adjust the cooking time.*

ONE OF THE MANY BASIL VARIETIES, THAI BASIL IS OFTEN DESCRIBED AS HAVING A SPICIER FRAGRANCE THAN SWEET BASIL. I'VE COMBINED IT WITH GINGER, LEMONGRASS, AND STEAMED MUSSELS FOR A DISH THAT IS FULL OF AROMATIC CHARACTERISTICS AND BROTHY RICHNESS.

• • •

STEAMED MUSSELS IN THAI BASIL COCONUT BROTH

2 teaspoons vegetable oil

1 tablespoon minced ginger

2 teaspoons minced garlic

¼ teaspoon dried red pepper flakes

1 tablespoon minced fresh lemongrass (optional)

1 (13.5 ounce) can unsweetened coconut milk

2 teaspoons Thai fish sauce (*nam pla*)

2 teaspoons soy sauce

3 tablespoons coarsely chopped fresh Thai basil

1 tablespoon fresh lime juice

2 pounds fresh mussels in the shell, washed and debearded

½ cup matchstick-cut carrots

½ cup matchstick-cut red bell pepper

¼ cup slivered green onion

1 tablespoon chopped fresh cilantro

In a large soup pot or Dutch oven, heat the oil over medium heat until hot. Add the ginger, garlic, red pepper flakes, and lemongrass and cook, stirring often, for about 30 seconds; do not let the mixture burn.

Add the coconut milk, fish sauce, soy sauce, Thai basil, lime juice, mussels, carrots, red peppers, and green onions. Bring to a boil, and cover immediately. Steam the mussels, covered, for 3 to 5 minutes, or until the mussels just open. Immediately remove from the heat. With a slotted spoon, divide the mussels (discard any that are unopened) and vegetables among bowls and pour the broth over them. Sprinkle with cilantro and serve immediately.

CHEF'S TIPS:
If Thai basil is not available, substitute any fresh basil.

THESE CHEESY GOUGÈRES ARE DELICIOUS AND SO RETRO-FRENCHY. THEY ARE ADDICTIVE LITTLE MORSELS TO POP AS YOU SIP A CHILLED GLASS OF BUBBLY.

• • •

PARMESAN POPPY SEED CHEESE PUFFS

½ cup water

½ cup whole milk

6 tablespoons butter

½ teaspoon salt

1 teaspoon minced garlic

1 cup flour

4 large eggs

¾ cup plus 1 tablespoon grated high-quality Parmesan

2 teaspoons poppy seeds

Place the water, milk, butter, salt, and garlic in a heavy, medium-sized saucepan. Bring to a boil over medium-high heat.

All at once, add the flour, stirring it in quickly with a wooden spoon. Keep stirring—the mixture will come away from the sides of the pan and become thick and stiff. Continue stirring and turning over the mixture for about 1 minute. (You want to dry the mixture out a bit.)

Transfer the mixture to a mixing bowl and, with a hand-held or standing mixer, beat on medium-high speed. Add 1 of the eggs.

CHEF'S TIPS:

● *If you're making lots of these puffs, you'll want to invest in a tiny commercial #70 scoop, available at restaurant supply stores. When using it, dip the scoop in cool water each time so the dough balls release easily.*
● *If you're short of baking sheets, have more dough balls ready on sheets of parchment. When a batch of puffs is done, remove the baking sheet from the oven, pull off the parchment filled with cooked puffs, and quickly place a waiting parchment sheet of dough balls onto the baking sheet.*

As soon as the egg is partially incorporated, increase the mixer speed to high. Add the remaining 3 eggs, ONE AT A TIME when each previous egg is well incorporated. The mixture should be smooth.

Set the dough aside for 5 minutes, then stir in ¾ cup of the Parmesan.

Let the dough cool completely, then cover and refrigerate it for 1 hour or up to 2 days before using.

Preheat the oven to 400°F. Line baking sheets with parchment paper. You will need 2 or 3 baking sheets, or work in batches. (If you don't have parchment paper, lightly spray the baking sheets with nonstick vegetable spray and watch the bottoms of the cheese puffs closely to prevent overbrowning.) Drop the dough by heaping teaspoonsful—they should be the size of large marbles—onto the parchment.

Mix together the poppy seeds and remaining 1 tablespoon grated Parmesan. Sprinkle the top of each dough ball with a little of the mixture.

Bake on the upper rack of the oven for 22 to 25 minutes, or until the puffs are golden. Serve warm.

You can make these a few hours in advance, keep them at room temperature, and then reheat them in a hot oven for a few minutes.

Makes 6 servings

I KNOW, THERE ARE A MILLION INGREDIENTS IN THIS RECIPE—BUT IT'S WORTH IT! YOU CAN PREPARE ALL OF THE COMPONENTS THE DAY BEFORE, AND THEN ASSEMBLE THE TOWERS THE DAY YOU PLAN TO SERVE THEM.

. . .

CRAB TOWERS

AVOCADO & HEARTS OF PALM MIXTURE

¼ teaspoon ground coriander

1 tablespoon lime juice

1 tablespoon olive oil

⅛ teaspoon salt

¼ teaspoon white pepper

2 avocados, cut into ¼-inch dice, pits reserved

½ cup diced canned hearts of palm, rinsed and drained well

CRAB MIXTURE

8 ounces high-quality crabmeat, well drained

3 tablespoons mayonnaise

1 tablespoon White Wine Vinaigrette (recipe follows)

GAZPACHO SALSA

2 tablespoons (⅛-inch dice) red bell pepper

2 tablespoons (⅛-inch dice) yellow bell pepper

(continued)

Read through the entire recipe before beginning any preparation. Prepare the White Wine Vinaigrette (page 65) first.

To make the Avocado & Hearts of Palm Mixture: In a bowl, whisk together the coriander, lime juice, olive oil, salt, and white pepper until well mixed. Gently fold in the avocado and hearts of palm until coated. Add a whole avocado pit to the mixture to prevent browning. Cover and refrigerate.

To make the Crab Mixture: In a bowl, mix together all ingredients until just combined. Cover and refrigerate.

To make the Gazpacho Salsa: In a bowl, combine all of the ingredients. Cover and refrigerate.

To assemble the towers: Lay 6 pieces of waxed paper, each approximately 4 inches square, on a baking pan. Place a 2½-inch-high by 2-inch-wide metal ring on each piece of paper. (See the Chef's Tip for a PVC option.) Divide the Avocado & Hearts of Palm Mixture among the rings, gently pushing it into place with the bottom of a clean, narrow glass or bottle that fits inside the ring. Next, add the Crab Mixture, dividing it evenly among the rings and gently pushing it into place. Then divide the Gazpacho Salsa evenly among the rings and press it down. Chill the towers thoroughly, for at least 2 hours or for up to 8 hours before serving.

¼ cup (⅛-inch dice) peeled,
seeded cucumber

2 tablespoons
(⅛-inch dice) seeded
Roma tomatoes

2 tablespoons (⅛-inch dice)
peeled lime segments
(all white pith and
membranes removed)

2 tablespoons (⅛-inch dice)
peeled orange segments
(all white pith and
membranes removed)

2 tablespoons
(⅛-inch dice) celery

1 tablespoon (⅛-inch
dice) red onion

1½ teaspoons finely
chopped fresh cilantro

1 tablespoon olive oil

¼ teaspoon salt

GARNISHES

1 cup baby frisée,
rinsed and spun dry

1½ tablespoons White
Wine Vinaigrette
(recipe follows)

1 tablespoon very
thinly sliced chives

To serve: Slip a spatula between each tower and its waxed paper and transfer it, still in the ring, to a large plate. With the glass or bottle you used to press down the mixture in the rings, gently and carefully press down on each tower and pull the ring up and away from each tower.

Mix the frisée with the White Wine Vinaigrette, tossing until coated. Place a pouf of the frisée on top of each tower. Sprinkle with the chives.

THIS RECIPE MAKES MORE THAN YOU WILL NEED FOR THE CRAB TOWERS. IT WILL KEEP, REFRIGERATED, FOR UP TO 2 WEEKS. ENJOY IT ON SEASONAL GREENS.

Makes about 1 cup • • •

WHITE WINE VINAIGRETTE

¼ cup white wine vinegar

¾ teaspoon salt

1 teaspoon minced lemon zest

½ teaspoon Dijon mustard

½ cup olive oil

¼ cup vegetable oil

In a small bowl, whisk all ingredients together to combine. (Whisk again as needed before using.)

CHEF'S TIPS:

If you don't happen to have half a dozen expensive French metal timbale rings, you can make the towers in PVC pipe! Go to your friendly hardware store and proceed to flirt shamelessly with the orange-apron-clad "associates." Ask them to cut your 10-foot by 2-inch interior diameter PVC pipe into 2½-inch sections. Then, once back at home with your bag of "tower molds," use a piece of fine sandpaper to remove any rough edges. Wash thoroughly before using.

(Do not use PVC rings for baking.)

THIS IS THE BEST THING TO NIBBLE WITH A MARTINI EVER!

· · ·

SESAME CHEDDAR
OLIVE POPPERS

1 cup (4 ounces) finely grated sharp Cheddar cheese

2 tablespoons butter, softened

½ cup sifted flour

Dash cayenne

1 jar (20 to 25) medium-large pimento-stuffed olives, drained

⅓ cup mixed white and black sesame seeds

Preheat the oven to 400°F.

Beat the cheese and butter together, in a mixer or food processor, until smooth. Stir in the flour and cayenne. Shape 1 heaping tea-spoon of dough around each olive, covering it well and shaping the dough into a ball. Place the sesame seeds in a small bowl. Roll each ball in the sesame seeds and place on an ungreased baking sheet. Bake for approximately 15 minutes. Serve hot.

CHEF'S TIPS:

● *You can make the dough for poppers in advance and refrigerate it for up to 1 week, or freeze it for up to 1 month.*
● *There is definitely a trick to wrapping these easily—but practice makes perfect. The olives can be wrapped in dough and tossed in sesame seeds up to 8 hours before baking, but not more. You can, however, bake these up to 1 day in advance and reheat them right before serving.*

Makes 15 appetizers

SURE, THEY TAKE LONGER, BUT THESE HOMEMADE CRACKERS ARE BET-
TER THAN STORE-BOUGHT SIMPLY BECAUSE IT'S FUN TO MAKE YOUR
OWN CRACKERS AND TO IMPRESS YOUR FRIENDS BY TELLING THEM
SO! THEN THERE'S THE OLD CLICHÉ OF GETTING TO ENJOY THE
FRUITS—OR IN THIS CASE, THE CRACKERS—OF YOUR LABOR. YOU WILL
NEED A PASTA MAKER FOR THIS RECIPE.

· · ·

SMOKED SALMON WITH WASABI CREAM CHEESE & GINGER PICKLED ONIONS ON HOMEMADE CRACKERS

1½ to 2 teaspoons wasabi powder (depending on how spicy you like it)

1½ tablespoons water

4 ounces reduced-fat or regular cream cheese, softened

15 pieces Homemade Crackers (recipe follows)

4 ounces hot-smoked salmon (or substitute cold-smoked or lox-style slices)

½ cup well-drained Ginger Pickled Onions (recipe follows)

2 tablespoons finely sliced fresh chives

In a small bowl, stir together the wasabi powder and water to make a smooth paste. Stir in the softened cream cheese and mix until smooth.

Dividing it evenly among the Homemade Crackers, spread some of the wasabi cream cheese onto each cracker. Top with the smoked salmon, then the Ginger Pickled Onions. Sprinkle with chives.

CHEF'S TIPS:
- *Bring the cream cheese to room temperature before making the wasabi cream cheese.*
- *Be sure to purchase only small amounts of wasabi powder, as it quickly goes stale and becomes bitter in taste.*

HOMEMADE CRACKERS

1 cup flour

½ teaspoon salt

1 teaspoon sugar

1 tablespoon butter, cut into small pieces

4 to 6 tablespoons milk

Flour for dusting

Kosher salt

Seeds, such as poppy or sesame, optional

Preheat the oven to 350°F.

In a food processor, mix together the flour, salt, sugar, and butter. Pulse until the mixture resembles coarse meal. With the machine running, gradually add the milk (add 4 tablespoons at first and, if the dough is dry, add more, 1 tablespoon at a time). Process until the dough comes together.

Remove the dough to a piece of plastic wrap and let it rest for 30 minutes or up to 1 hour before proceeding.

Transfer the dough to a lightly floured surface and divide into 8 pieces.

Press the dough into a disk to fit a pasta machine. Run the dough through the machine several times, each time reducing the setting from largest to smallest. Do this until the dough is cracker-thin (about ⅛ inch). You can also roll the dough by hand—it just takes some muscle! When rolling by hand, roll the dough into long, rectangular pieces that are cracker-thin or ⅛ inch thick.

Place the rolled-out pieces on large baking sheets lined with parchment paper, and lightly mist or brush them with water. Sprinkle with kosher salt and the optional seeds.

Using a fork, prick the dough all over. Bake for 10 to 15 minutes, or until the crackers are lightly browned and crisp.

Cool. Break each cracker into about 4 pieces. Serve immediately or store at room temperature in a tightly covered container.

CHEF'S TIPS:
For a variety of interesting crackers, add lemon zest,
black pepper, or herbs to the dough.

THESE ONIONS ARE ALSO GREAT AS A GARNISH IN MARTINIS AND ON SANDWICHES. MAKE THEM AT LEAST 1 DAY BEFORE SERVING TO ENHANCE THE FLAVORS.

Makes 1½ cups   • • •

GINGER PICKLED ONIONS

2 tablespoons thinly shaved pink pickled ginger (the kind you get with sushi), chopped

1 red onion, sliced ⅛ inch thick

1 cup seasoned rice wine vinegar

¼ cup water

Place the ginger and onion in a small stainless steel bowl or heat-resistant glass container. Combine the remaining ingredients in a small noncorrosive saucepan and bring to a boil over high heat. As soon as the mixture is boiling briskly, pour it over the onions.

Push the onions down into the mixture with a spoon and let cool. When the mixture cools to room temperature, place a small, heavy plate or bowl directly on the onions to weigh them down. Cover with plastic wrap and refrigerate overnight.

Remove the plate or bowl after a day. Drain the liquid from the onions before serving. Onions will keep, refrigerated, for up to 1 month.

Makes about 40 crostini

CROSTINI CAN BE MADE IN ADVANCE, COOLED THOROUGHLY, AND STORED IN AIRTIGHT CONTAINERS FOR UP TO 3 DAYS. IF NECESSARY, RECRISP THEM IN A HOT OVEN FOR A COUPLE OF MINUTES. YOU CAN SERVE THESE CROSTINI AS IS OR WITH A NUMBER OF ADDITIONAL TOPPINGS (SEE THE CHEF'S TIPS).

• • •

HERBED CROSTINI

1 long, skinny French baguette, sliced on the diagonal into ¼-inch slices

Herb Oil as needed (recipe follows)

¾ teaspoon kosher salt

Preheat the oven to 400°F.

Lightly brush the baguette slices with Herb Oil, or place the slices in a large bowl, drizzle with Herb Oil, and toss well. Place the bread in a single layer on baking sheets, sprinkle with salt, and toast until just crispy. Let cool before storing.

Mix all ingredients together well. Store, refrigerated, for up to 10 days, or freeze for up to 3 months.

Makes 1 cup

• • •

HERB OIL

1 cup extra virgin olive oil

½ teaspoon dried basil leaves

½ teaspoon dried thyme leaves

½ teaspoon salt

Pinch cayenne

1 tablespoon minced garlic

Mix all ingredients together well. Store, refrigerated, for up to 10 days, or freeze for up to 3 months.

CHEF'S TIPS:

This is the "must have" party basic. Keep Herb Oil in the freezer along with a frozen baguette for emergency snacks. Topping variations are endless: goat cheese and roasted pepper, olive tapenade with cucumbers and feta, smoked salmon and chive cream. . . .

Makes 10 to 15 servings

OKAY, YOU'RE HAVING AN APPETIZER PARTY: YOU *GOTTA* HAVE SOME GOOEY CHEESE! A BIG SKILLET OF FETA TOPPED WITH LEMON, FENNEL, AND HERB-MARINATED OLIVES AND BAKED IN THE OVEN UNTIL MELTY—MMMMMMM, IT'S A TANTALIZING FLAVOR COMBINATION. THIS RECIPE IS SO EASY, AND IT'S WONDERFUL SERVED WITH PITA CHIPS OR SLICES OF RUSTIC BREAD. I SERVE THIS IN THE SAME IRON SKILLET I USE TO MAKE THE DISH.

• • •

SEXY BAKED OLIVES
& FETA CHEESE

1½ cups mixed imported olives, not pitted, drained (do not use oil-cured olives)

1 tablespoon chopped fresh thyme

2 teaspoons minced lemon zest

¼ teaspoon dried red pepper flakes

1 teaspoon fennel seeds

2 tablespoons extra virgin olive oil

1 thick (7- to 8-ounce) piece feta cheese

Pita Chips (recipe follows), optional

In a small bowl, toss the olives with the thyme, lemon zest, red pepper flakes, fennel seeds, and olive oil.

Lightly oil the bottom of an 8- to 9-inch ovenproof skillet, such as cast iron.

Place the cheese in the center of the pan, then top with the marinated olive mixture. Use a rubber spatula to get all the goodies out of the olive-tossing bowl and onto the cheese. Some olives will stay on top of the cheese and some will fall to the side. At this point, you can cover and refrigerate the skillet for up to 1 day.

When ready to bake, preheat the oven to 400°F.

Bake the cheese and olives for about 20 minutes, or until the cheese is soft and gooey. Serve immediately, right out of the pan, with slices of rustic bread, crostini, pita, or Pita Chips.

PITA CHIPS

3 tablespoons olive oil

1 teaspoon dried basil leaves, crumbled

¾ teaspoon kosher salt

6 large whole wheat pita breads (about 12 ounces total), each cut in 8 wedges

Preheat the oven to 450°F.

In a large bowl, combine the olive oil, basil, and salt. Add the cut-up pita wedges and toss well, coating them evenly with the oil mixture.

On 2 large baking sheets, spread out the pita wedges in a single layer. Bake for about 4 minutes, then turn the pieces over and continue baking for 4 to 5 more minutes, or until golden and crisp.

The chips can be made in advance, cooled thoroughly, and stored in airtight containers for up to 3 days. If necessary, recrisp them in a hot oven for a couple of minutes.

CHEF'S TIPS:

● *French feta is a mild, creamy cheese and is really my favorite to use in this recipe.*

● *This recipe can easily be multiplied for a large crowd.*

STUFFED MUSHROOMS ARE A PARTY FOOD CLASSIC. HERE THEY'RE REBORN WITH SASSY BLUE CHEESE AND TOASTY HAZELNUTS.

• • •

BLUE CHEESE & HAZELNUT–STUFFED MUSHROOMS

30 large (1½-inch-diameter) mushrooms, about 1 pound

1 tablespoon butter

¼ cup finely chopped onion

2 teaspoons minced garlic

1 teaspoon minced fresh thyme

2 tablespoons dry sherry

¼ teaspoon salt

½ cup cream

Dash Tabasco

¼ teaspoon Worcestershire

¼ cup toasted hazelnuts (page 25), finely chopped

¼ cup (1 ounce) crumbled blue cheese

3 tablespoons grated high-quality Parmesan

2 tablespoons dry unseasoned bread crumbs

Remove the stems of the mushrooms; set the caps aside. Finely chop the mushroom stems.

In a large nonstick skillet, melt the butter over medium-high heat. Add the chopped mushroom stems and onion and sauté for 3 to 4 minutes, or until the mushrooms are soft. Add the garlic and sauté for 30 seconds. Add the thyme, sherry, and salt, and cook until the mixture is dry. Add the cream, Tabasco, and Worcestershire. Cook, stirring often, until the cream is reduced and thickened and the liquid is almost all cooked out. The mixture should be paste-like.

Remove from the heat, transfer the mixture to a bowl, and let it cool to room temperature. When cool, stir in the toasted chopped hazelnuts, blue cheese, Parmesan, and bread crumbs.

Stuff the mushroom caps, dividing the filling evenly among them (about 2 teaspoons per mushroom). Press the filling in well and mound it up.

Lightly spray a rimmed baking sheet with nonstick vegetable spray, or oil it with olive oil. Place the mushrooms, not touching, on the baking sheet. (If desired, cover tightly and refrigerate for up to 1 day. Let come to room temperature before baking.)

Preheat the oven to 400°F. Bake the mushroom caps for about 10 minutes, or until they are just getting tender and lightly browned and the filling is gooey. Serve immediately.

CHEF'S TIPS:
Sprinkle the greased baking pan lightly with salt and pepper before placing the mushroom caps on the pan to season the bottoms of the mushrooms.

Makes 8 to 12 servings

THE CITRUS IN CEVICHE "COOKS" THE FISH WITH ACID RATHER THAN WITH HEAT. ALTHOUGH THE TEXTURE OF THE FISH CHANGES, AND IT TURNS FROM TRANSLUCENT TO OPAQUE, THE FISH ESSENTIALLY REMAINS RAW, SO SELECT QUALITY FISH TO ENSURE SAFETY. FOR LARGE PARTIES, I LIKE TO SERVE THIS CEVICHE IN SHOT GLASSES WITH TINY COCKTAIL FORKS.

• • •

TROPICAL CEVICHE

MARINADE

½ cup fresh lime juice

1½ teaspoons minced lime zest

½ cup rice vinegar

2 tablespoons sugar

½ to ¾ teaspoon dried red pepper flakes

1 teaspoon salt

1 teaspoon coriander seed, crushed or coarsely ground

CEVICHE

½ pound bay scallops, or substitute thinly sliced or quartered sea scallops

6 ounces boneless, skinless, VERY FRESH firm fish, such as halibut or snapper

½ small red onion, cut in half crosswise and thinly sliced lengthwise

2 tablespoons coarsely chopped fresh cilantro

1 cup (½-inch dice) mango or papaya

¾ cup (½-inch dice) fresh pineapple

Combine the marinade ingredients in a large glass or stainless steel mixing bowl. Whisk together and set aside.

Rinse the scallops and fish quickly and gently in cold water and pat dry with paper towels. Add the scallops to the marinade and refrigerate. Working quickly, dice the fish into ½-inch pieces, then add them to the marinade with the onion.

Cover and refrigerate for at least 4 hours before serving. Stir occasionally to ensure that the marinade penetrates the seafood evenly. The ceviche can be prepared to this point up to 2 days in advance.

Half an hour before serving time, stir the cilantro and fruits into the ceviche, and return the dish to the refrigerator until ready to serve.

STARTERS

Spiced Squash Bisque

Shaved Fennel & Arugula Salad
with Lemon Vinaigrette

Charlotte's Greek Grilled Pita Salad

Warm Spinach Salad with Shiitake Mushrooms,
Sweet Peppers & Sesame Honey Dressing

Shrimp Won Ton Soup with Lemongrass

Gala Apple, Blue Cheese & Toasted Pecan
Salad with Cider Vinaigrette

Seasonal Greens with Spicy Walnuts,
Crisp Asian Pears & Cranberry Vinaigrette

Butter Lettuce & Endive Salad with Avocado,
Grapefruit & Pomegranate Seeds

Wedge O'Lettuce with Retro Dressings
Green Goddess Dressing
Blue Cheese & Beer Dressing
Spicy Chipotle "French" Dressing

Baby Greens with Blackberry-Honey
Vinaigrette, Toasted Hazelnuts & Chèvre

Best of the Season Gazpacho

ORGANIC OR HOMEGROWN SQUASH IS PREFERABLE IN THIS RECIPE BECAUSE IT CREATES A MUCH MORE PRONOUNCED AND SWEET FLAVOR. I LIKE TO USE HUBBARD, DANISH, OR BUTTERNUT SQUASH, OR A COMBINATION. MAKE THE CRISPY SEEDS WHILE THE SOUP IS COOKING.

• • •

SPICED SQUASH BISQUE

3 tablespoons olive oil

1 cup diced onion

4½ cups (about 1½ pounds) peeled, seeded, and cubed winter squash (any combination of sweet squash or pumpkin can be used; reserve ¼ cup seeds for Crispy Seeds)

2 cloves garlic, minced

1 teaspoon coriander seeds, finely crushed

1 teaspoon cardamom seeds, finely crushed

1½ teaspoons ground cumin

¼ teaspoon ground nutmeg

¼ teaspoon cayenne

1 bay leaf

1½ teaspoons salt (more or less, depending upon whether you are using a homemade stock)

3 cups chicken stock

¾ cup sour cream

Crispy Seeds (recipe follows)

In a large, heavy saucepan, heat the olive oil over medium-high heat. Add the onion and sauté for 2 to 3 minutes. Add the squash, garlic, spices, bay leaf, and salt. Sauté for 2 to 3 minutes. Add the chicken stock and bring to a boil. Turn down the heat, partially cover the pan, and simmer for 15 to 20 minutes, or until the squash is very tender.

Remove the bisque from the heat. Remove and discard the bay leaf. In a blender or food processor, carefully purée the hot soup in small batches with the sour cream. (Be careful not to make your batches too large, since the soup is very hot.) Taste for seasoning and add salt as needed, especially if using homemade stock. Pour the puréed soup back into the pan and keep warm.

Divide the soup among warmed soup bowls. Sprinkle each serving with about 2 teaspoons Crispy Seeds.

For a vegetarian version: Substitute vegetable stock for the chicken stock.

CRISPY SEEDS

¼ cup seeds from squash

1½ teaspoons olive oil

¼ teaspoon ground cumin

1 teaspoon sugar

⅛ teaspoon salt

Preheat the oven to 375°F. Rinse the seeds under cold water to remove any squash flesh or strings. Drain well and measure. Place in a bowl and toss with the olive oil. In a small bowl, combine the cumin, sugar, and salt and sprinkle over the seeds. Toss well and spread the seeds on a nonstick baking sheet. Roast for 8 to 10 minutes, or until crispy and toasted.

CHEF'S TIPS:

For a fun and impressive presentation, thin a small amount of sour cream with milk or cream until it is a "squeezable" consistency and put it in a squirt bottle. Swirl the top of each serving of bisque with the sour cream.

SIMPLE FLAVORS BLEND FOR A CLASSIC SALAD.

• • •

SHAVED FENNEL & ARUGULA SALAD WITH LEMON VINAIGRETTE

1 large fennel bulb

1 teaspoon minced lemon zest

3 tablespoons fresh lemon juice

3 tablespoons extra virgin olive oil

¼ teaspoon salt

8 cups baby arugula or regular arugula, torn into bite-sized pieces, washed and spun dry

1 small head radicchio, cut into bite-sized pieces, washed and spun dry

Freshly ground black pepper

Cut off and discard the fennel stalks from the top of the bulb. Cut the bulb in half lengthwise and cut out the core. Cut each half in half again to make quarters. Starting from the end of a quarter, cut ⅛-inch half-moons, or "shavings," as thin as possible. Place in a bowl of ice water and let stand to crisp for at least 10 minutes or up to 2 hours. Spin dry before tossing them in the salad.

Place the lemon zest and lemon juice in a large bowl. Slowly whisk in the olive oil and then the salt. Add the shaved fennel, arugula, and radicchio, and toss the salad. Season with freshly ground black pepper and serve immediately.

CHEF'S TIPS:

● *This recipe is for a large party, but you can cut it in half for a smaller number of servings.*

● *For super-thin shaved fennel, use a Japanese mandoline. Available at Asian grocers, this piece of equipment is one of my very few kitchen gadgets. It's exceptionally useful and, best of all, very affordable.*

Makes 6 to 8 starter servings
or 4 entrée servings

MY SOUS-CHEF CHARLOTTE RUDGE HAS CONTRIBUTED HER FAVORITE TWIST ON ONE OF MY FAVORITES, BREAD SALAD. INSTEAD OF USING CHUNKS OF RUSTIC ITALIAN BREAD, SHE GRILLS PITA BREAD (THE KIND WITHOUT POCKETS), THEN SLICES IT AND COMBINES IT WITH GREEK SALAD MUSTS. FOR A PRETTY TWIST, ADD YELLOW TEARDROP TOMA-TOES OR, IF HEIRLOOM TOMATOES ARE IN SEASON, A VARIETY OF DIFFERENTLY COLORED TOMATOES. SUPER DELICIOUS, AND A GREAT SALAD TO DO WHEN YOU'RE GRILLING!

• • •

CHARLOTTE'S GREEK GRILLED PITA SALAD

3 tablespoons red wine vinegar

6 tablespoons extra virgin olive oil

Pinch dried red pepper flakes

1 teaspoon minced garlic

½ teaspoon salt

⅓ cup (2 ounces) crumbled feta cheese

1 tablespoon chopped fresh oregano

2 (7-inch) pita breads— without pockets

2 large vine-ripe tomatoes, cut in wedges

1 cup thinly sliced Walla Walla Sweet or red onion

1 large cucumber, peeled and sliced crosswise

⅓ cup pitted kalamata olives, cut in half

¼ cup coarsely chopped Italian parsley

Preheat the grill.

In a large bowl, whisk together the vinegar, olive oil, pepper flakes, garlic, salt, cheese, and oregano. Set aside.

Place the whole pitas on the hot grill and cook on each side for about 1½ minutes, or until nice grill marks form and the pitas are toasty. Remove and cut each pita in half and then into 1-inch strips.

Add the tomatoes, onion, cucumber, olives, parsley, and grilled pita strips to the bowl of vinaigrette and toss together well. Serve immediately.

Makes 6 starter servings or
4 entrée servings

THIS RECIPE IS EASY TO ASSEMBLE ONCE YOU HAVE ALL THE ELEMENTS READY. THE INGREDIENTS CAN BE PREPARED UP TO 2 DAYS IN ADVANCE. FOR AN ENTRÉE SALAD, ADD SLICES OF SMOKED CHICKEN OR DUCK OR BARBECUED PORK.

• • •

WARM SPINACH SALAD WITH SHIITAKE MUSHROOMS, SWEET PEPPERS & SESAME HONEY DRESSING

2 large bunches fresh spinach (4 quarts), washed and dried

2 tablespoons vegetable oil

2 teaspoons minced garlic

1 cup very thinly sliced shiitake mushrooms (you can substitute button mushrooms or create a combination)

½ cup very thinly sliced red onion

¾ cup very thinly sliced mixed red and yellow bell peppers

¾ cup Sesame Honey Dressing (recipe follows)

1 tablespoon toasted sesame seeds

1 package enoki mushrooms for garnish, optional

Pick the stems from the spinach, wash the leaves, drain well, and spin dry. Place the spinach in a large bowl.

In a large sauté pan, heat the oil over medium-high heat until hot. Add the garlic, shiitake mushrooms, onion, and bell peppers. Sauté for a couple of minutes, then add the Sesame Honey Dressing. Stir well and heat until just hot. Pour the mixture over the spinach in the bowl. Sprinkle with the sesame seeds and toss to coat the spinach leaves well.

Divide the salad among serving plates and garnish with enoki mushrooms, if desired. Serve immediately.

SESAME HONEY DRESSING

¼ cup honey

2 tablespoons molasses

¼ cup Dijon mustard

¾ cup rice vinegar

1¼ cups vegetable oil

¼ cup Asian-style sesame oil

1 tablespoon minced ginger

1½ teaspoons minced garlic

½ teaspoon *sambal oelek* or other hot chile sauce (or substitute ¼ teaspoon dried red pepper flakes)

1 teaspoon salt

In a large bowl, whisk together the honey, molasses, Dijon mustard, and vinegar. Slowly whisk in the oils until emulsified. Whisk in the ginger, garlic, *sambal oelek*, and salt. Cover and refrigerate until needed. Whisk well before using.

Extra dressing can be kept for up to 1 month, refrigerated.

CHEF'S TIPS:

Fresh spinach is sometimes very muddy! Here's how I prepare it. Cut the stems off all at once, with a sharp knife, while the spinach is still bundled. Fill a clean sink with cool water, gently plunge the leaves into the water, and stir them around. Remove the spinach to a colander and drain the sink, being sure to rinse out all mud and sand. Refill the sink and wash the leaves again. Return the leaves to a colander to drain, then spin dry. You can prepare the leaves up to 3 days in advance if they're kept covered well and refrigerated.

GROUND CHICKEN, PORK, OR CRABMEAT MAY BE SUBSTITUTED FOR THE SHRIMP.

SHRIMP WON TON SOUP WITH LEMONGRASS

WON TONS

8 ounces raw shrimp meat

1 tablespoon soy sauce

1½ teaspoons very finely minced ginger

½ teaspoon salt

1½ teaspoons minced garlic

1 green onion, chopped

24 won ton skins

SOUP

8 cups rich chicken stock, preferably homemade

1 tablespoon soy sauce

2 teaspoons minced ginger

1 tablespoon minced fresh lemongrass

½ cup thinly sliced strips of barbecued pork, optional

½ cup thinly sliced carrots

½ cup thinly sliced celery

1 small leek (white part only), thinly sliced and rinsed well

1 baby bok choy, thinly sliced

Minced green onion

To make the won tons: Place the shrimp, soy sauce, ginger, salt, garlic, and green onion in a food processor. Process until well combined. Divide the filling among the won ton skins. Dip your fingers in water and lightly dampen the edge of one won ton skin. Fold, in normal won ton fashion (the directions should be on the won ton package). Repeat until all of the won tons are folded. Refrigerate, covered, until needed.

To make the soup: In a large pot, combine the chicken stock, soy sauce, ginger, and lemongrass. Taste the soup at this point and add salt if necessary. (If you are using purchased chicken broth, the soup will probably be salty enough, but if you are using homemade stock, season generously.) Bring to a slow boil and add the won tons. Be careful that the soup does not boil too hard, or the won tons will break open. Cook for about 2 minutes, then add the pork, carrot, celery, leek, and bok choy. Bring back to a slow boil and cook for another 3 to 4 minutes, or until the won tons are just tender. Divide the soup among warmed bowls and sprinkle with green onion.

CRISPY, FLAVORFUL GALA APPLES COME INTO PLAY IN THIS SALAD. SKIN-ON SLICES JOIN GOURMET GREENS, BLUE CHEESE, AND TOASTED PECANS—AND ARE QUICKLY TOSSED WITH A CIDER VINAIGRETTE SPIKED WITH MUSTARD AND SWEETENED WITH APPLE JUICE.

• • •

GALA APPLE, BLUE CHEESE & TOASTED PECAN SALAD WITH CIDER VINAIGRETTE

CIDER VINAIGRETTE

3 tablespoons apple juice concentrate

3 tablespoons cider vinegar

1 tablespoon Dijon mustard

¼ cup olive oil

•

½ cup pecan pieces

2 Gala apples

9 cups gourmet mixed greens or a mixture of seasonal lettuces and cut romaine leaves, washed and spun dry

½ heaping cup crumbled blue cheese

⅓ cup dried cranberries, coarsely chopped

To make the Cider Vinaigrette: Whisk together the apple juice concentrate, cider vinegar, and mustard. Gradually whisk in the olive oil. Refrigerate until needed.

Preheat the oven to 350°F. Place the pecans on a baking sheet and toast until just golden, 5 to 7 minutes. Set aside to cool.

When ready to serve, quarter each apple (leave the skin on), core, and then slice into ⅛-inch to ¼-inch slices. Toss well in a large bowl with the greens, blue cheese, and about half the dressing. Divide among 6 chilled, oversized dinner plates, then sprinkle each salad with toasted pecans and dried cranberries. Serve immediately. Pass the remaining dressing separately.

CHEF'S TIPS:
● *Make a quadruple batch of the vinaigrette for other uses. It will keep, refrigerated, for up to 3 weeks.*
● *This recipe is also great made with toasted hazelnuts or walnuts.*
● *Try this recipe with your other favorite apples, like Granny Smith, or even slices of Anjou or Bartlett pear.*

Makes 4 to 6 servings

MY ABSOLUTE FAVORITE SALAD! THE UNIQUE DRESSING HAS A BEAUTIFUL RUBY RED COLOR AND A SWEET AND TANGY FLAVOR THAT'S A PERFECT COUNTERBALANCE TO THE SPICY WALNUTS AND REFRESHING ASIAN PEARS. I LOVE TO SERVE THIS BRIGHT AND FESTIVE SALAD DURING THE HOLIDAYS.

• • •

SEASONAL GREENS WITH SPICY WALNUTS, CRISP ASIAN PEARS & CRANBERRY VINAIGRETTE

SPICY WALNUTS

1½ teaspoons butter, melted

⅛ teaspoon cayenne

⅛ teaspoon ground cinnamon

2 tablespoons honey

¼ teaspoon salt

½ cup coarsely chopped walnuts

•

8 cups mixed seasonal greens

1 large or 2 small Asian pears, quartered, cored, and sliced into ⅛-inch wedges

½ small red onion, thinly sliced

Cranberry Vinaigrette (recipe follows)

To make the Spicy Walnuts: Combine all of the walnut ingredients in a small skillet and toss well to coat. Cook over medium heat until the nuts are lightly browned. Remove from the heat and let cool, stirring frequently to keep the nuts from sticking together.

To assemble the salad: Toss the seasonal greens, Asian pear, and onions with some of the Cranberry Vinaigrette until well coated. Divide among individual salad plates. Top the salads with Spicy Walnuts and pass the extra vinaigrette.

88 | Dishing with Kathy Casey

● ● ●

CRANBERRY VINAIGRETTE

⅔ cup fresh or frozen cranberries

¼ cup sugar

½ cup white wine or distilled vinegar

1 teaspoon Dijon mustard

¼ cup orange juice

¾ cup vegetable oil or very light olive oil

¼ teaspoon salt

¼ teaspoon black pepper

Place the cranberries, sugar, and vinegar in a small saucepan. Cook over medium heat until the cranberries pop, 4 to 5 minutes. Remove from the heat and let cool. Purée the cranberry mixture in a blender.

Pour the purée into a medium bowl and whisk in the mustard and orange juice. Gradually whisk in the oil, a little at a time. The dressing should become smooth and emulsified. Season with salt and pepper. Refrigerate until needed.

CHEF'S TIPS:
Make a lot of this dressing and bottle it for wonderful holiday hostess gifts. Be sure to tell guests to keep it refrigerated. It is so good you will want to pour it over everything, including slices of leftover cold turkey!

Makes 2 servings

• • •

THIS ELEGANT SALAD IS PERFECT FOR A ROMANTIC DINNER FOR TWO.

BUTTER LETTUCE & ENDIVE SALAD WITH AVOCADO, GRAPEFRUIT & POMEGRANATE SEEDS

CHAMPAGNE VINAIGRETTE

2 teaspoons champagne vinegar (or substitute white wine vinegar)

1½ tablespoons olive oil

½ teaspoon Dijon mustard

1 teaspoon minced fresh tarragon

Pinch salt

Pinch black pepper

•

1 small Ruby Red grapefruit

½ head butter lettuce

½ small head Belgian endive

½ avocado

2 tablespoons pomegranate seeds

To make the Champagne Vinaigrette: In a small bowl, whisk together all of the vinaigrette ingredients. Cover and refrigerate until ready to serve. You can make the vinaigrette up to 1 day in advance.

Cut the peel and all the white pith from the grapefruit, exposing the flesh. With a small paring knife, cut out the grapefruit segments. Set aside 6 segments for the salad and reserve the remainder for another use.

Wash the lettuce and spin it dry. Use mainly the inner leaves of the butter lettuce, tearing larger leaves into bite-sized pieces if necessary. Cut the "root" end off the Belgian endive, then peel off each leaf. Arrange the leaves in a stack and cut them in half lengthwise.

Peel the avocado half and slice it lengthwise into 8 to 12 thin slices. (The remaining avocado half can be kept, with the pit, wrapped and refrigerated, for 1 or 2 days.)

Toss the lettuce and endive with 1 tablespoon of the Champagne Vinaigrette. Divide between 2 oversized dinner plates. Arrange the avocado slices and 3 grapefruit segments atop the greens. Drizzle the remaining vinaigrette over the salad. Scatter each plate with pomegranate seeds. Serve immediately.

CHEF'S TIPS:

This salad is geared more toward the fall and winter, with its combination of Ruby Red grapefruit and pomegranate seeds. For a wonderful summer version, replace the grapefruit with an orange and the pomegranates with raspberries or blackberries that have been cut in half.

Makes 4 servings

FOR MANY OF US BOOMERS, ICEBERG WEDGE SALADS WERE OUR FIRST "GREEN SALADS." IS ICEBERG OBSOLETE? NO WAY! IT'S A VERY CRISPY LETTUCE THAT DOESN'T EASILY GET SOGGY OR LIMP. WITH MY MODERN VERSIONS OF RETRO DRESSINGS AND DELISH GARNISHES, EVEN LETTUCE SNOBS ARE WON OVER.

• • •

WEDGE O'LETTUCE WITH RETRO DRESSINGS

1 small head iceberg lettuce, washed, dried, and cut into quarters

Dressing and garnish of your choice (options follow)

Make the dressing in advance and prepare the garnishes as needed.

To assemble the salad: Place a wedge of lettuce on each of 4 dinner-sized plates. Top each wedge with ¼ cup of dressing. Sprinkle the garnishes on top or arrange them stylishly around the plate. Pass extra dressing at the table.

Makes 2 cups

• • •

GREEN GODDESS DRESSING

1 ripe avocado, peeled and pitted (reserve pit)

2 egg yolks

¼ cup fresh lemon juice

2 tablespoons thinly sliced fresh chives

2 tablespoons minced parsley

2 tablespoons minced fresh tarragon

1 shallot, minced

4 anchovy fillets

⅓ cup olive oil

½ cup sour cream

¼ teaspoon black pepper

¼ teaspoon salt

In a food processor, place the avocado, egg yolks, lemon juice, herbs, shallot, and anchovies and process for 1 minute until well combined. With the machine running, slowly drizzle in the oil. The mixture should become smooth and creamy. Turn the machine off and scrape down the sides. Add the sour cream, pepper, and salt and process for 30 seconds more.

Place the mixture in a container and submerge the avocado pit in it to help the dressing keep its green color. Lay a piece of plastic wrap directly on the dressing's surface and cover well. The dressing will keep, refrigerated, for up to 4 days.

(continued)

4 large radishes, sliced

½ cup thinly sliced English cucumber, with skin

Thinly sliced fresh chives

Makes 2 cups   • • •

BLUE CHEESE & BEER DRESSING

1 cup mayonnaise

½ cup sour cream

½ cup (2 ounces) crumbled blue cheese

1 tablespoon very finely minced onion

¾ teaspoon minced garlic

1½ teaspoons chopped Italian parsley, optional

½ teaspoon Worcestershire

¼ teaspoon salt

¼ teaspoon black pepper

¼ teaspoon Tabasco

¾ teaspoon fresh lemon juice

2 tablespoons beer or ale

GARNISHES

8 ounces cooked bay shrimp

4 to 6 slices bacon, cooked crispy and crumbled

2 hard-boiled eggs, chopped

¼ cup slivered almonds, toasted

Place all ingredients except the garnishes in a food processor. Pulse until the ingredients are mixed and the cheese chunks are slightly broken up but not puréed.

Refrigerate, covered, for up to 10 days.

SPICY CHIPOTLE "FRENCH" DRESSING

2 tablespoons diced onion

1 teaspoon minced garlic

1½ teaspoons chipotle pepper purée (page 25)

1 tablespoon dry mustard

½ cup sugar

1 teaspoon salt

½ teaspoon black pepper

1 tablespoon paprika

⅔ cup cider vinegar

½ cup tomato-based chili sauce, such as Heinz Chili Sauce

½ cup vegetable oil

2 tablespoons olive oil

GARNISHES

1 small, sweet white onion, such as Vidalia or Walla Walla Sweet

1 tablespoon white wine or distilled vinegar

2 cups cold water

1½ teaspoons sugar

2 large vine-ripe beefsteak tomatoes

1 tablespoon chopped fresh cilantro or parsley

To make the dressing: In a blender or food processor, process all the dressing ingredients until smooth and emulsified. Refrigerate until needed. The dressing will keep for 2 weeks, refrigerated.

To make the garnish: Slice the onion into ¼-inch slices. In a glass or stainless steel bowl, combine the vinegar, water, and sugar, then toss in the sliced onion. Make sure the onion is covered by the liquid. Cover and refrigerate for at least 1 hour and up to 4 hours. When ready to serve, drain the onions well and cut the tomatoes into ¾-inch dice. Scatter onion rings and diced tomatoes over lettuce wedges. Sprinkle with cilantro or parsley.

Makes 4 servings

ONE OF MY VERY FAVORITE SEASONAL SALAD COMBINATIONS IS FLUFFY BABY GREENS WITH A LUSCIOUS, TANGY BERRY DRESSING. I LOVE THE PLAY OF THIS SWEET AND TANGY DRESSING AGAINST THE CRISP GREENS AND CRUNCHY HAZELNUTS, BALANCED WITH CREAMY CHÈVRE AND THE TWANG FROM THOSE FRESH, TART BERRIES. THIS DRESSING IS ALSO GREAT MADE WITH RASPBERRIES.

• • •

BABY GREENS WITH BLACKBERRY-HONEY VINAIGRETTE, TOASTED HAZELNUTS & CHÈVRE

BLACKBERRY-HONEY VINAIGRETTE

¼ **cup fresh or frozen blackberries**

2 **tablespoons red wine vinegar**

1 **tablespoon honey**

1 **teaspoon Dijon mustard**

3 **tablespoons canola oil or light olive oil**

Pinch cayenne pepper

¼ **teaspoon kosher salt**

•

8 **cups mixed baby greens**

½ **cup fresh blackberries or raspberries**

¼ **cup (1 ounce) chopped, toasted hazelnuts (page 25)**

2 **ounces chèvre-style goat cheese, crumbled**

To make the Blackberry-Honey Vinaigrette: Combine all the vinaigrette ingredients in a blender or food processor and process until smooth. Refrigerate until needed. The vinaigrette can be made up to 3 days in advance.

To assemble the salad: Toss the greens with the Blackberry-Honey Vinaigrette and divide among 4 plates. Scatter with berries, hazelnuts, and goat cheese. Serve immediately.

CHEF'S TIPS:
If berries are out of season, substitute frozen berries in the dressing and omit the fresh berries in the salad.

· · ·

BEST OF THE SEASON GAZPACHO

1½ teaspoons minced garlic

¼ cup diced sweet white onion, such as Vidalia or Maui

1 cup peeled, seeded, and diced cucumber

½ cup diced green bell pepper

¼ cup coarsely chopped fresh cilantro

¼ cup coarsely chopped Italian parsley

1½ cups diced rustic bread (crusts removed)

3 cups diced ripe tomatoes

⅓ cup thinly sliced celery

½ cup extra virgin olive oil

1 to 2 tablespoons sherry vinegar

1½ teaspoons sugar

1½ cups water

2 teaspoons salt

¼ teaspoon black pepper

¼ teaspoon dried red pepper flakes

GARNISHES

Tiny teardrop tomatoes

Cilantro leaves

In a large bowl, combine all ingredients except garnishes. (Start with 1 tablespoon of the sherry vinegar, make the soup, then add more vinegar later if more acidity is desired.)

In 3 or 4 batches, process the ingredients in a food processor or large blender until almost puréed. Gazpacho should still have some texture. Mix all processed batches together and chill in a noncorrosive (plastic, glass, or stainless steel) container for at least 4 hours or overnight.

Serve in chilled bowls. Garnish each bowl with a sprinkle of tiny tomatoes and cilantro, if desired.

MAINS

Roasted Shrimp with Thai Lime Butter

Seared Steak with Chipotle
Mushrooms & Crema

Grilled Halibut with Lemon-Herb Splash

Herb-Marinated Grilled Chicken Breasts

Roasted Beef Tenderloin for a Crowd with
Horseradish Mustard Crust

Crab Soufflé Cakes with Sweet
Pepper & Corn Relish

Chardonnay Braised Chicken

Roasted King Salmon with
Orange-Ginger Salsa

Roasted Pork Loin with Fennel Spice Rub

Roasted Vegetable Risotto

"Stinking Rose" Clam Pasta

Seared Lamb with Olive Jus
& Minted Herb Salad

New Century Lobster Américaine
Poached in Herb Butter

Makes 4 servings

LIME'S BRIGHT FLAVOR NOTE SHINES WITH THE ACCOMPANYING MINT, CILANTRO, AND LEMONGRASS IN THIS RECIPE.

• • •

ROASTED SHRIMP WITH THAI LIME BUTTER

16 to 20 large (size 8/12 or U-12) shrimp, in the shell

Salt and black pepper

½ recipe Thai Lime Butter, softened to room temperature (recipe follows)

Preheat the oven to 475°F.

Split each shrimp lengthwise down the middle of the back but do not cut them all the way through. Open the shrimp flat to "butterfly" them, and season them lightly with salt and pepper. Smear the inside meat of each shrimp with about 2 teaspoons of Thai Lime Butter. Place the shrimp 1 inch apart on a rimmed baking sheet. Roast for about 6 minutes, or until just barely done. The shrimp will continue to cook slightly once removed from the oven. Serve immediately.

Makes 1½ cups

• • •

THAI LIME BUTTER

½ pound (2 sticks) butter

2 teaspoons minced lime zest

¼ cup fresh lime juice

1 tablespoon very finely minced lemongrass

2 tablespoons chopped fresh mint

2 tablespoons chopped fresh cilantro

¼ teaspoon dried red pepper flakes

2 tablespoons minced ginger

¼ teaspoon curry powder

2 teaspoons minced garlic

1 tablespoon Thai fish sauce (*nam pla*)

Combine the ingredients in a mixer or food processor and process until well combined. Store, tightly covered and refrigerated, for up to 1 week, or freeze for 3 months.

Extra Thai Lime Butter can be rolled into a log, wrapped thoroughly in plastic wrap, and frozen for up to 3 months. Slice off a few pieces as needed. Here are some of my favorite uses:

• For oven-roasted fish fillets: Put about 2 tablespoons on each fillet of mild fish, such as halibut or ling cod, before roasting in a hot 400°F oven.

• For grilled tuna or seared sea bass: Bring the butter to room temperature and smear it on fish right after removing it from the heat.

• For steamed clams or mussels: Add about 2 tablespoons of the butter and ¼ cup dry white wine to each pound of clams or mussels. Place them in a large pot, cover, and cook until they just open.

READ THIS RECIPE ALL THE WAY THROUGH BEFORE BEGINNING.
PREPARE THE CHIPOTLE MUSHROOMS & CREMA FIRST.

• • •

SEARED STEAK WITH CHIPOTLE MUSHROOMS & CREMA

1 teaspoon salt

¼ teaspoon ground cumin

¼ teaspoon ground coriander

½ teaspoon dried oregano

¼ teaspoon black pepper

4 (8- to 10-ounce) sirloin steaks

Vegetable oil as needed

Chipotle Mushrooms & Crema (recipe follows)

Cilantro sprigs for garnish

In a small bowl, mix the salt, cumin, coriander, oregano, and black pepper. Season the steaks evenly on each side with the spice mixture, patting it into the steak surfaces.

Meanwhile, drizzle a little oil into a large skillet. Heat the oil over medium-high to high heat until quite hot. Sear the steaks on the first side until browned and half cooked, turn them over, and continue cooking until the desired doneness is reached. (Do not crowd the steaks in the pan. Cook them in batches if necessary.) Cooking times will vary with the thickness of steaks.

Top each steak with warm Chipotle Mushrooms & Crema. Garnish with sprigs of cilantro.

CHEF'S TIPS:

Pan-searing steaks is a smoky business, but it's worth it for the incomparable crusty surface that is so delish. Just be sure to turn your kitchen fan on full blast.

Makes 2 cups

● ● ●

CHIPOTLE MUSHROOMS & CREMA

2 tablespoons butter

1 cup thinly sliced
white onion

6 cups sliced mushrooms
(use a mixture of white
mushrooms and wild
mushrooms if in season,
such as chanterelles,
porcini, etc.)

1 tablespoon minced garlic

1 teaspoon dried oregano

¼ teaspoon ground
coriander

1 teaspoon salt

¼ teaspoon black pepper

1½ teaspoons chipotle
pepper purée (page 25)

¼ cup chicken or
mushroom stock

3 tablespoons gold tequila

¾ cup cream

1 tablespoon
fresh lime juice

2 tablespoons coarsely
chopped fresh cilantro

In a large, heavy skillet, melt the butter over medium-high heat. Add
the onion and sauté for 3 minutes, then add the mushrooms and garlic and cook, stirring occasionally, until the mushrooms and onions
are tender, 3 to 4 minutes. Stir in the oregano, coriander, salt, and
black pepper. Mix the chipotle purée into the stock. Add the stock
mixture and tequila to the skillet and cook, reducing until only a little
liquid remains, about 5 minutes.

Add the cream and cook until the mixture is slightly thickened and
the cream is reduced. Stir in the lime juice and cilantro just before
serving.

Makes 4 to 6 servings IF GRILLING IS NOT YOUR THING, YOU CAN PAN-SEAR OR BAKE THE FISH. SEA BASS IS A DELICIOUS ALTERNATIVE TO THE HALIBUT. THE LEMON-HERB SPLASH ALSO MAKES A GREAT MARINADE FOR GRILLED PRAWNS OR SEA SCALLOPS.

• • •

GRILLED HALIBUT WITH LEMON-HERB SPLASH

LEMON-HERB SPLASH

6 tablespoons extra virgin olive oil

2 tablespoons fresh lemon juice

2 teaspoons minced lemon zest

1½ teaspoons minced fresh rosemary

1½ teaspoons minced fresh basil

1 tablespoon minced parsley

⅛ teaspoon dried red pepper flakes

½ teaspoon minced garlic

¼ teaspoon salt

•

4 (6-ounce) halibut steaks or fillets

Oil as needed

Salt and black pepper

To make the Lemon-Herb Splash: Mix all ingredients together well and refrigerate until needed.

Preheat the grill until hot. Lightly rub the fish on each side with a little oil and season with salt and pepper as desired.

Grill the fish for 2 to 3 minutes per side, depending on the thickness of the fish. The fish should be nicely grill marked and cooked through but still juicy.

Place the halibut on plates and splash each piece of fish with 1 tablespoon or more of the Lemon-Herb Splash. Pass the remaining splash on the side.

CHEF'S TIPS:
To add a light smoky flavor, soak a few wood chips, such as apple, mesquite, or pecan (depending upon where you live), in water, and throw them on the coals just before placing the fish on the grill.

Makes 6 servings THIS FULL-FLAVORED MARINADE ADDS A QUICK POW TO EVERYDAY CHICKEN BREASTS. IT IS ALSO GREAT ON FISH, SHRIMP, AND EVEN GRILLED PORTOBELLO MUSHROOMS.

• • •

HERB-MARINATED GRILLED CHICKEN BREASTS

HERB MARINADE

3 tablespoons olive oil

1½ tablespoons balsamic or sherry vinegar

1½ tablespoons finely grated or minced lemon zest

1½ tablespoons minced fresh thyme

1½ tablespoons minced fresh chives

1 tablespoon minced fresh rosemary

⅛ teaspoon dried red pepper flakes

•

6 boneless skinless chicken breasts

1 to 1½ teaspoons kosher salt

Chopped fresh chives and herb sprigs, optional

In a medium bowl, whisk together the marinade ingredients. Rub the marinade on the chicken breasts, coating each piece of chicken well. Refrigerate for at least 1 hour or up to overnight.

Preheat the grill. When ready to cook, season each side of the breasts with a generous sprinkling of kosher salt. Grill the chicken over medium coals or flame until marked on each side and the internal temperature reaches 160°F, about 5 minutes per side, depending on how hot your grill is. (The chicken will gain another 5°F off the grill.)

Garnish with chopped fresh chives and herb sprigs if desired.

CHEF'S TIPS:

• *Make a triple batch of the marinade and freeze it for quickie single meals. Just chip out a tablespoon per breast as you need it. (Or freeze it in 1-tablespoon cubes in ice cube trays.) The marinade will keep, frozen, for up to 2 months.*

• *Cook extra chicken to thinly slice for sandwiches or to top a Caesar salad for lunch*

Makes 10 to 14 servings

IN RESTAURANTS, THE CRISPY, SALTY, FATTY OUTSIDE PIECES THAT FALL OFF WHEN SLICING PRIME RIB ARE CALLED "SCOOBY SNACKS." THESE PIECES ARE COVETED AND FOUGHT OVER BY THE COOKS! I CREATE SOMETHING SIMILAR AT HOME WITH THIS RECIPE.

• • •

ROASTED BEEF TENDERLOIN FOR A CROWD WITH HORSERADISH MUSTARD CRUST

HORSERADISH MUSTARD CRUST

3 tablespoons prepared horseradish

3 tablespoons whole-grain mustard

2 tablespoons kosher salt

1½ teaspoons coarsely ground black pepper

4 cloves garlic, peeled

1 large shallot, peeled and cut in quarters

2 teaspoons minced fresh thyme

¼ cup olive oil

•

1 large (about 5 pounds) whole beef tenderloin, trimmed*

*Tuck the skinny end under and tie, or ask your butcher to do this for you. Also ask him to lightly trim the meat of any fat.

Preheat the oven to 400°F. Place a rack in a shallow roasting pan.

To make the Horseradish Mustard Crust: In a food processor, process all the ingredients until a paste is formed. Dry the beef tenderloin well with paper towels, then smear the paste all over it.

Place the roast on the roasting rack, and place the pan in the oven. Roast to the doneness you like. A meat thermometer inserted into the center of a beef roast registers 120°F for rare and 130°F for medium-rare. For a 5-pound tenderloin, allow about 45 minutes to 1 hour for medium-rare. The temperature will increase as the meat "rests" before carving.

Remove the roast from the oven and loosely tent it with foil; let it stand for 10 minutes before carving so the juices don't run out. Carve the slices across the grain.

CHEF'S TIPS:
The crust on this is pretty flavorful, so a sauce isn't really needed. If you like, stir a dollop of prepared horseradish into unsweetened, lightly whipped cream and serve alongside.

THESE ARE GREAT AS A MAIN DISH, BUT I ALSO LIKE TO SERVE THEM AS
A STARTER OR SMALL PLATE, OR I'LL MAKE TINY INDIVIDUAL ONES TO
USE AS A COCKTAIL APPETIZER FOR LARGER CROWDS. READ THE
ENTIRE RECIPE BEFORE STARTING.

• • •

CRAB SOUFFLÉ CAKES WITH SWEET PEPPER & CORN RELISH

**Sweet Pepper & Corn Relish
(recipe follows)**

⅓ cup buttermilk

**½ cup fresh or frozen
corn kernels**

2 large eggs

1 teaspoon fresh lime juice

¼ teaspoon Tabasco

½ teaspoon salt

½ teaspoon baking powder

⅓ cup yellow cornmeal

¼ cup flour

**8 ounces high-quality
crabmeat, preferably fresh,
such as Dungeness or lump**

2 green onions, minced

1 tablespoon olive oil

GARNISHES

¼ cup sour cream

4 sprigs cilantro

4 lime wedges

Make the Sweet Pepper & Corn Relish first.

Place the buttermilk and corn in a blender and blend on high speed
for 30 seconds, or until the mixture is smooth.

Separate the eggs, reserving the whites. In a medium bowl, combine
the yolks with the buttermilk-corn mixture, lime juice, Tabasco, and
salt, mixing well.

Sift together the baking powder, cornmeal, and flour. Add to the buttermilk mixture and combine well.

Drain any excess juice from the crab and add the crab to the batter,
along with the green onions. Stir lightly.

Right before serving, beat the egg whites until softly peaked but not
dry. Gently fold into the batter.

Heat a 10-inch nonstick skillet over medium heat until hot (droplets
of water sprinkled in the pan will sizzle). Add the olive oil to the pan
and swirl it around, coating the pan well. Spoon heaping table-
spoonsful of batter into the pan, cooking 3 to 4 cakes at a time, or as
many as your pan allows. Cook the cakes until lightly golden, approximately 1½ minutes, then flip and continue cooking until golden on
the second side and the cakes have started to puff lightly. Continue
cooking the cakes in batches, adding more oil if necessary.

For entrée servings, spoon ¼ cup of Sweet Pepper & Corn Relish onto the center of a warm dinner plate and place 3 crab cakes around the relish. Top each cake with a tiny dollop of sour cream. Garnish each plate with a sprig of cilantro and a lime wedge.

Makes 1 cup • • •

SWEET PEPPER & CORN RELISH

1 slice bacon, minced (or omit and increase olive oil to 1 tablespoon)

2 teaspoons olive oil

½ cup (¼-inch dice) red bell pepper

½ cup (¼-inch dice) red onion

1 teaspoon minced garlic

¾ cup fresh or frozen corn kernels

2 tablespoons fresh lime juice

1½ tablespoons packed brown sugar

⅛ teaspoon cayenne

Tiny pinch dried red pepper flakes

¼ to ½ teaspoon salt

1 green onion, minced

2 tablespoons chopped fresh cilantro

In a 10-inch, nonstick skillet over medium-high heat, cook the bacon until crisp, approximately 2 minutes. Add the olive oil, red pepper, red onion, and garlic to the pan and sauté for 2 minutes, or until the mixture is just beginning to soften. Add the corn and sauté for another 1 to 2 minutes. Add the lime juice, brown sugar, cayenne, red pepper flakes, and salt, and remove from the heat. Let cool to room temperature, then stir in the green onion and cilantro.

CHEF'S TIPS:
● *If using lump crabmeat, be sure to pick through it and check for pieces of shell before mixing it in.*
● *These cakes need to be made just before serving, so the beaten egg whites that are folded in stay fluffy.*

Makes 4 to 6 servings

I AM NOT ONE TO CONFORM, BUT IN THIS CASE, I HAVE CAVED IN FOR FLAVOR'S SAKE. ALMOST A TEXTBOOK PAIRING, CHARDONNAY AND CHICKEN ARE BEAUTIFUL TOGETHER WHEN SLOWLY OVEN-BRAISED WITH TOASTED FENNEL SEED, MUSHROOMS, PEPPERS, THE "ORIGINAL TRIO" (CARROT, CELERY, AND ONION), AND THYME. RICH AND PER-FUMED, THIS PREPARATION IS FINISHED WITH FRESH HERBS AND A LITTLE CREAM TO CREATE AN ELEGANT DISH.

• • •

CHARDONNAY BRAISED CHICKEN

2 tablespoons olive oil

1 large (about 4 pounds) chicken, cut into 8 pieces— 2 breasts, 2 legs, 2 thighs, 2 wings

1 teaspoon salt

¼ teaspoon black pepper

1 teaspoon fennel seed

¾ cup large-diced onion

¾ cup large-diced celery

¾ cup large-diced carrot

¾ cup sliced mushrooms

¾ cup large-diced red bell peppers

1 tablespoon minced garlic

1 teaspoon minced fresh thyme

1¾ cups chardonnay

1 tablespoon water

1 tablespoon cornstarch

¼ cup cream

1 tablespoon minced fresh chives

1 tablespoon minced Italian parsley

Preheat the oven to 350°F.

In an ovenproof braising pan, large Dutch oven, or wide soup pot, heat the olive oil over high heat.

Meanwhile, lay the chicken pieces out on a baking sheet and sprinkle both sides with the salt and pepper.

When the oil is hot, brown the chicken pieces well, about 4 minutes on each side, doing it in 2 batches if necessary. Remove the browned chicken to a plate.

Reduce the heat to medium-high, add the fennel seed and onion to the pan, and cook for about 10 seconds. Add the celery, carrot, mushrooms, and bell pepper and cook, stirring often, for 2 to 3 minutes, or until lightly browned. Stir in the garlic, and cook for 30 seconds more.

Place the chicken back in the pan, tucking it between the vegetables. Add the thyme and the wine. Bring to a boil, then cover.

Place in the oven and cook for 30 minutes. Remove the lid and cook for another 30 minutes, or until the chicken is very tender. Remove the chicken and vegetables to a platter and keep warm.

Measure the liquid; you should have about 2 cups. Place the pan, with the liquid, over medium-high heat. (If you have more than 2 cups of liquid, boil it for a minute or so to reduce it.) In a small cup, mix together the water and cornstarch. Whisk this mixture into the liquid in the pan, and add the cream. Cook, whisking continuously, until the liquid comes to a boil. Boil for about 2 minutes, or until saucy. Remove the pan from the heat, stir in the chives and parsley, and spoon the sauce over the chicken and vegetables.

CHEF'S TIPS:

- *You must have heard the following saying many times by now: "If you wouldn't drink it, then don't cook with it." The flavor of your wine is the flavor that is imparted to the dish you are cooking.*
- *If you are feeling a little rebellious, make this with a petite sirah or Côtes du Rhone.*

Makes 4 servings

I LOVE THAI SWEET CHILI SAUCE—IT IS A SWEET AND SOMEWHAT HOT SAUCE THAT HAS A TRANSLUCENT QUALITY AND IS WONDERFUL IN ALL KINDS OF DISHES. I MIX IT WITH MAYO TO DOLLOP ON CRAB CAKES OR SPREAD ON GRILLED CHICKEN SANDWICHES. BE SURE YOU PURCHASE SWEET CHILI SAUCE AND NOT THE HOT VARIETY. SOMETIMES THIS INGREDIENT IS LABELED THAI SWEET CHILI SAUCE "FOR CHICKEN" IN THE STORE; IT MAY HAVE A PICTURE OF A CHICKEN ON THE LABEL.

• • •

ROASTED KING SALMON
WITH ORANGE-GINGER SALSA

4 (6- to 8-ounce) thick, boneless, skinless salmon fillets

Salt and black pepper

2 tablespoons olive oil

¼ cup Spicy Orange-Ginger Butter (recipe follows)

Orange-Ginger Salsa (recipe follows)

Black sesame seeds, toasted, optional

Make the Spicy Orange-Ginger Butter and Orange-Ginger Salsa first.

Preheat the oven to 450°F.

Season the salmon on each side with salt and pepper. Heat the olive oil in a large skillet until hot. Place the salmon flesh side down in the skillet and sear over medium-high heat until lightly golden. Turn the salmon over and sauté about a minute more. Place the pan of salmon in the oven until the fish is just done and slightly opaque in the center. (The timing will vary depending on the thickness of your salmon, so check it often. It shouldn't take more than a couple of minutes.)

Place each piece of salmon on a warm plate and top with a table-spoon of Spicy Orange-Ginger Butter. Then top each piece with a heaping ¼ cup of Orange-Ginger Salsa. Sprinkle lightly with black sesame seeds, if desired, and serve immediately.

SPICY ORANGE-GINGER BUTTER

8 tablespoons (1 stick) butter, softened, cut into chunks

2 teaspoons minced orange zest

¾ teaspoon *sambal oelek*

2 tablespoons Thai sweet chili sauce

2 tablespoons orange juice concentrate

1 teaspoon sugar

2 teaspoons soy sauce

1 tablespoon very finely minced ginger

2 tablespoons fresh lime juice

1 green onion, thinly sliced

Place all ingredients except the green onion in a food processor. Process until smooth and emulsified, scraping down the sides of the work bowl often. (If it doesn't come together right away, be patient and continue processing.) When the mixture is well blended, add the green onion and pulse until mixed.

Keep refrigerated, tightly covered, for up to 7 days, or freeze for up to 4 months for use throughout the salmon season.

ORANGE-GINGER SALSA

¾ cup (¼-inch dice) orange (peeled and seeded)

¾ cup (¼-inch dice) Roma tomatoes

1½ teaspoons minced ginger

2 tablespoons (¼-inch dice) sweet white onion

1½ teaspoons fresh lime juice

1½ teaspoons olive oil

1½ teaspoons minced fresh cilantro

¼ teaspoon salt

¼ teaspoon ground coriander

½ teaspoon sugar

1 tablespoon Thai sweet chili sauce

Mix all ingredients together well.

Makes 6 to 8 servings   WITH THIS RECIPE, THE ROASTED PORK PAN JUICES AND DRIPPINGS STIRRED WITH SOUR CREAM MAKE FOR A DELICIOUS SAUCE ACCOMPANIMENT, NOT TO MENTION THE GREAT FLAVOR COMBINATION OF FENNEL AND ORANGE. . . . ZOWIE!

• • •

ROASTED PORK LOIN WITH FENNEL SPICE RUB

1 (2½-pound) boneless pork top loin roast, tied

FENNEL SPICE RUB

1 tablespoon fennel seed, crushed well

2 tablespoons minced orange zest

2 teaspoons dried thyme leaves

¼ teaspoon dried red pepper flakes

1 large shallot, peeled and quartered

2 teaspoons kosher salt

1 tablespoon Dijon mustard

2 tablespoons olive oil

SAUCE

¼ cup water

½ cup white wine

½ cup sour cream

1½ teaspoons cornstarch

2 tablespoons water

Preheat the oven to 350°F. Place a rack in a shallow roasting pan. Pat the pork roast dry with paper towels.

In a food processor, combine the rub ingredients and process until finely chopped. Smear the pork on all sides with the rub, being sure to use it all. For more intense flavor penetration, rub the roast up to 4 hours before cooking.

Place the roast on the rack in the roasting pan and cook for 1½ to 1¾ hours, or until a meat thermometer inserted into the center registers 160°F.

Remove the roast from the pan to a platter to rest for 10 minutes before carving while you make the sauce.

Place the hot roasting pan on a burner and add the water and wine, scraping up all the pan drippings from the bottom of the pan. Bring to a boil, then reduce to a simmer and whisk in the sour cream.

Whisk together the cornstarch and water in a small cup, and then whisk it into the sauce. Cook until the sauce is thickened and has come to a boil. Remove from the heat. Thinly slice the pork and serve with the sauce.

CHEF'S TIPS:
The rub is also wonderful smeared on pork chops before grilling or on a whole chicken before roasting.

RISOTTO—NOW DON'T LET THAT SCARE YOU. . . . IT'S A GREAT DISH, BUT WHO WANTS TO STAND IN FRONT OF THE STOVE FOREVER IN THE MIDDLE OF DINNER? MY RECIPE CALLS FOR MAKING A RISOTTO BASE AS MUCH AS 3 DAYS IN ADVANCE.

• • •

ROASTED VEGETABLE RISOTTO

¼ cup (about 2 ounces) chopped pancetta

1 tablespoon olive oil

1½ teaspoons minced garlic

1 cup diced Roma tomatoes

¼ cup dry white wine

About 1¾ cups chicken stock

Risotto Base (recipe follows)

Roasted Vegetables (recipe follows)

4 tablespoons (½ stick) butter, cut into small pieces

½ cup grated high-quality Parmesan, plus extra for garnish

2 tablespoons chopped fresh basil

1 teaspoon minced fresh rosemary

1 teaspoon minced fresh marjoram

Salt and black pepper

Fresh herb sprigs for garnish

Cook the chopped pancetta in a sauté pan over medium heat until crispy. Drain on paper towels.

In a wide, heavy saucepan, heat the olive oil over medium-high heat and sauté the garlic and tomatoes for just a few seconds, being careful not to brown the garlic.

Add the white wine and stock, and bring to a boil. Immediately stir in the Risotto Base and Roasted Vegetables. Stirring often, let the risotto reduce to a creamy but still brothy consistency, about 5 minutes. (The risotto should be heated through at this point.) If it gets too thick, add a little more stock.

Turn off the heat and immediately stir in the butter, Parmesan, and chopped herbs. Taste the risotto and season as needed with salt and black pepper.

Divide the risotto among warm bowls and sprinkle with a little grated Parmesan and the crisp pancetta. Garnish with extra Parmesan and fresh herb sprigs.

For a lighter or vegetarian version: Omit the pancetta, decrease the butter to 2 tablespoons, and decrease the Parmesan to ¼ cup. Make the Roasted Vegetable Risotto and Risotto Base with vegetable or mushroom stock.

• • •

RISOTTO BASE

3 cups homemade chicken stock, lightly salted, or 2 cups canned stock plus 1 cup water

1 tablespoon olive oil

1 cup chopped mushrooms

1½ teaspoons minced garlic

1 tablespoon minced shallots

1½ cups arborio rice

¾ cup dry white wine

In a saucepan, heat the chicken stock until simmering. Lower the heat and keep the stock warm. Do not boil or reduce it.

In a wide, heavy saucepan, heat the olive oil over medium-high heat. When the oil is hot, add the mushrooms. Cook until lightly sautéed, about 3 minutes.

Add the garlic, shallots, and rice. Cook for about 1 minute, stirring constantly. Reduce the heat to medium and add the white wine. Cook until the wine is almost totally absorbed, stirring often, about 1 minute.

Stir in one-third of the warm stock. Simmer slowly, stirring often and adjusting the heat if necessary, until the liquid is almost totally absorbed, about 6 minutes.

Stir in another third of the stock. Simmer slowly, stirring often, until the liquid is almost totally absorbed, 6 to 8 minutes. Stir in the remaining stock. Simmer slowly, stirring often, until the liquid is almost totally absorbed, 6 to 8 minutes more.

The rice should now be al dente in texture (firm to the bite) but a bit creamy in consistency. Immediately remove the pan of rice from the heat and spread the rice out on a baking sheet. Let cool at room temperature for 15 to 20 minutes. When totally cooled, place in a container with a tight-fitting lid and refrigerate until needed, up to 3 days.

• • •

ROASTED VEGETABLES

**1 medium Japanese
eggplant, sliced in half
lengthwise and then
sliced crosswise into
½-inch half-moons**

**1 medium red bell pepper,
cut into 1-inch dice**

**1½ cups quartered button
mushrooms and/or sliced
portobello mushrooms**

1 cup (1-inch dice) red onion

1 tablespoon olive oil

¼ teaspoon salt

Preheat the oven to 500°F.

Place the vegetables in a large bowl and drizzle with the olive oil. Sprinkle with the salt and toss everything together well. Spread the vegetables out on a baking sheet and bake for 18 to 20 minutes, or until the vegetables are browned on the edges and just tender.

Let cool to room temperature. Place in a container, cover, and refrigerate until needed, up to 2 days.

CHEF'S TIPS:
*Never, never make risotto using regular long-grain white rice. Arborio rice
will give you that "creamy" risotto texture so key to the dish. Always
purchase a high-quality brand arborio rice because you'll get better
results than you will with an inexpensive brand.*

AS FAR AS I KNOW, GARLIC IS USED IN JUST ABOUT EVERY CUISINE—
EXCEPT MAYBE SCANDINAVIAN BLAND-LAND. HEY! I CAN SAY THAT—
I AM SCANDINAVIAN! I COULD NOT IMAGINE THIS DISH WITHOUT A BIG
GARLIC PUNCH. IN THIS RECIPE, YOU WILL DEFINITELY GET A GOOD
DOSE!

• • •

"STINKING ROSE" CLAM PASTA

8 ounces dry linguini

**Olive oil and kosher salt
for pasta**

**3 tablespoons extra
virgin olive oil**

**1½ pounds fresh clams
(scrubbed and rinsed)**

**2 tablespoons
minced garlic**

**2 (6¼-ounce) cans
chopped clams with juice**

2 tablespoons lemon juice

¼ cup white wine

1 tablespoon cornstarch

**1½ teaspoons chopped
fresh oregano**

**1 tablespoon
chopped parsley**

**4 tablespoons (½ stick)
butter, cold, cut into
small chunks**

Right before making the sauce, cook the pasta according to the
package directions, until just al dente. Drain it well, toss it very lightly
with a splash of olive oil and salt to taste, then place it on a large
platter and cover tightly with plastic wrap to keep warm.

Heat the olive oil in a large sauté pan over medium-high heat. Add
the fresh clams and garlic, and sauté, but do not brown the garlic.
Add the canned clams with their juice and the lemon juice, increase
the heat to high, cover the pan, and cook until the clam shells just
open, about 2 minutes.

When the clams have opened, carefully remove them and place on
top of the pasta, being careful to keep the clam meats in their shells.
Re-cover with plastic wrap to keep warm.

Meanwhile, in a small bowl, whisk together the wine and cornstarch
to make a slurry. Whisk the slurry into the pan juices and bring to a
quick boil to thicken. Stir in the fresh herbs. Add the butter, a chunk
at a time, whisking after each addition, until the butter is just melted.
After adding the last chunk of butter, immediately remove the sauce
from the heat and pour over the clams and pasta.

CHEF'S TIPS:

*Before cooking, check to make sure your clams are still
alive and fresh by pinching closed the shells of any open ones. If they
snap closed, they are still good; if they don't close but stay
open, they should be tossed.*

GETTING MULTIPLE INGREDIENTS TOGETHER AHEAD OF TIME IS CALLED *MISE EN PLACE,* AND IT'S THE WAY RESTAURANT CHEFS CAN PUT OUT ALL THOSE SPECTACULAR DINNERS SO FAST. THAT IS WHAT YOU WILL WANT TO DO WITH THE RED WINE GLAZE, MINT OIL, AND HERB SALAD FOR THIS RECIPE. THEN YOU CAN JUST DRIZZLE, POUF, AND SERVE AT THE LAST MINUTE.

• • •

SEARED LAMB WITH OLIVE JUS & MINTED HERB SALAD

Olive Compound (recipe follows)

Herb Salad (recipe follows)

Mint Oil (recipe follows)

Red Wine Glaze (recipe follows)

6 thick (5-ounce) lamb chops or tenderloins, or a 2-pound piece of boneless, trimmed loin

Kosher salt and freshly cracked black pepper

About 3 tablespoons olive oil

1 cup chicken stock or demi-glace

Fresh mint sprigs for garnish

Prepare the Olive Compound, Mint Oil, and Red Wine Glaze in advance. Store them, refrigerated, then bring to room temperature before cooking the lamb. Prepare and mix the Herb Salad just before cooking the lamb. Cover with plastic wrap and refrigerate until ready to serve.

Preheat the oven to 475°F.

Season the lamb liberally on both sides with kosher salt and freshly cracked black pepper. Heat 1 tablespoon olive oil in a large, heavy skillet over medium-high to high heat. When the pan is very hot, place 2 or 3 pieces of lamb in the pan, being careful not to over-crowd them. Quickly sear the lamb on each side until browned, but do not cook it through. Remove the first batch of lamb to a rack on a rimmed baking sheet. Repeat with the remaining pieces, using additional olive oil as needed. Reserve the skillet for the next step. You can brown the lamb up to 1 hour before dinner and let it sit at room temperature before finishing.

Place the lamb in the oven and roast until medium, about 130°F internal temperature. (The temperature will continue to rise a little after roasting.)

Have the Olive Compound ready. Place the pan in which the lamb was browned over high heat, add the chicken stock or demi-glace, and reduce the liquid for 2 to 3 minutes, until the sauce is reduced to a glaze. Remove from the heat and vigorously whisk in the Olive Compound.

To serve: If using boneless loin or tenderloins, slice the lamb across the grain into thick medallions. Place the medallions or whole lamb chops on large warmed dinner plates. (If serving with risotto, mashed potatoes, or a similar accompaniment, divide it among the plates, placing it in the center. Cozy the lamb chop or medallions up against the accompaniment.) Spoon the olive pan sauce over the lamb. Place a pouf of Herb Salad on the lamb. Drizzle Mint Oil around each plate in a decorative, "artsy" fashion. Repeat with the Red Wine Glaze. Garnish each plate with a mint sprig. Serve immediately.

Makes ⅔ cup • • •

OLIVE COMPOUND

4 tablespoons (½ stick) butter, softened

1½ teaspoons Dijon mustard

1½ teaspoons minced fresh basil

¾ teaspoon minced fresh thyme

1 teaspoon minced garlic

1 teaspoon minced lemon zest

1 tablespoon finely chopped parsley

1 tablespoon minced shallot

¼ cup pitted kalamata olives, chopped

In a mixer or food processor, whip the butter with all of the ingredients except the olives until fluffy and well combined. Add the olives and mix until combined.

This recipe can be made in advance and refrigerated for up to 1 week or frozen for up to 1 month.

Makes 6 poufs

2 tablespoons tiny "hand-picked" pieces of curly parsley, washed and patted dry

2 tablespoons sliced (½-inch pieces) chives, washed and patted dry

2 tablespoons torn mint leaves, washed and patted dry

• • •

HERB SALAD

Mix the herbs together shortly before serving.

Makes ⅔ cup

1 bunch fresh mint, washed and chopped

Pinch kosher salt

¼ cup vegetable oil

¼ cup olive oil

• • •

MINT OIL

Place the mint and salt in a blender. Pour the vegetable oil on top. Blend, pausing as needed to mash and move the ingredients around. Add the olive oil, then blend again. Strain if the mixture is still really chunky (personally, I like to see some pieces of mint remaining), and place it in a squirt bottle. Refrigerate until needed. Do not leave at room temperature. This recipe can be made in advance and refrigerated for up to 1 week or frozen for up to 1 month.

Makes ¼ cup

1 (750 ml) bottle cabernet or other dry red wine

2 tablespoons sugar

• • •

RED WINE GLAZE

Place the wine and sugar in a noncorrosive saucepan and bring to a boil over medium-high heat, then reduce the heat to a simmer. Simmer the wine until reduced to a syrupy consistency, watching it closely in the last part of cooking. You should have ¼ cup. This will take about 1 hour. (Watch it carefully!) Cool the glaze and place it in a squirt bottle. This recipe can be made in advance and refrigerated for up to 1 month.

LOBSTER, ALWAYS A ROMANTIC DINNER FAVORITE, GETS LUCKY—WITH A SEDUCTIVE POACHING IN HERB BUTTER. IT MIGHT BE A LITTLE INTIMI-DATING TO COOK THESE GUYS, BUT THE TASTY MORSELS MAKE IT WORTH STEPPING OUT OF YOUR COMFORT ZONE.

• • •

NEW CENTURY LOBSTER AMÉRICAINE POACHED IN HERB BUTTER

2 (1- to 1½-pound) whole live lobsters

6 tablespoons butter, softened

3 tablespoons thinly sliced chives

½ teaspoon minced fresh thyme

2 teaspoons minced or grated lemon zest

2 tablespoons minced shallot

2 teaspoons minced garlic

1 teaspoon Dijon mustard

½ cup dry white wine, such as chardonnay, or Champagne

1 tablespoon brandy

1 tablespoon fresh lemon juice

1 tablespoon olive oil

½ cup thinly sliced very small leek, white part only, rinsed and drained well

½ cup thinly sliced mushrooms

Salt and black pepper

Purchase the lobsters the same day or the day before you'll be cooking them. Ask your seafood dealer about storing lobster before cooking. To prepare the lobsters, first be sure they are still alive. Keep the claws secured with rubber bands.

Have ready a large bowl or tub of ice and water. In a large pot, place enough water to immerse the lobsters completely. Bring the water to a full boil over high heat. Add the lobsters, and keep them immersed with tongs or a large spatula. Let the water return to a boil, then reduce the heat and simmer the lobsters for 5 minutes. Remove the lobsters and immediately plunge them into the ice bath. Let chill until they're cool enough to handle comfortably.

To clean the lobsters, break off the claws, with attached legs, and reserve. Pick up the lobster, underside up, holding the tail in one hand and the upper body in the other. Arch the lobster's back and twist it slightly to break the tail from the body. Bend back the tail flippers to break them off. Reserve the flippers for garnish, if desired.

Pick up the tail section, hard shell toward your palm, and squeeze it firmly to crack the softer undershell. Then, using both hands, break open the underside of the tail section lengthwise.

Carefully remove the tail meat in a single piece. Split it in half lengthwise; remove and discard the vein running down the tail.

To prepare the claws and attached legs, break the claw/leg sections apart at the joints. Crack the shells of the leg sections and, using a

10 red baby teardrop tomatoes

6 long chives for garnish

seafood pick or similar implement, pick out the meat and reserve. For the large claws, use a nutcracker or a mallet to crack the butt end of the claw shell in several places, taking care not to crush the meat. Remove the shell to expose the meat about halfway up the claws, but LEAVE THE PINCER SHELLS INTACT. This will preserve a red-shell look in the presentation.

Tightly cover and refrigerate the lobster meat. The recipe can be prepared to this point up to a day in advance.

Mix the butter, chives, thyme, lemon zest, shallot, garlic, and mustard together well. This step can be done up to 3 days in advance. Store, tightly covered and refrigerated. Be sure to let the butter mixture soften before using.

When ready to serve, mix the wine, brandy, and lemon juice together. Have all of the other ingredients ready. Warm 2 very large, shallow pasta bowls or oversized rimmed dinner plates. Place a 10- to 12-inch sauté pan over medium-high heat. Heat the olive oil, add the leek and mushrooms, and sauté for about 2 minutes. Season to taste with salt and pepper.

Add the wine mixture, raise the heat to high, and reduce the liquid by half. Lower the heat to medium, add the butter mixture in dollops, then arrange the lobster and baby tomatoes on top, reserving the flippers. Return to a simmer, cover the pan, and cook for 1 minute. Uncover the pan, turn the larger lobster pieces over, and cook just until the lobster is heated through and the liquid is somewhat reduced, about 2 minutes more.

To serve, remove the lobster tails and claws to a spare plate and cover with plastic wrap to keep warm. With a slotted spoon, divide the mushrooms, leeks, and smaller pieces of lobster meat between the 2 serving plates, mounding the mixture in the center. Arrange the lobster tails on top of the mixture, then place the claws and reserved flippers around them. Spoon the tomatoes and remaining sauce over and around the lobster. Garnish with long chive strands. Serve immediately.

• • •

SIDES

Grilled Asparagus with Hazelnut Aioli

Maple Scalloped Sweet Potatoes with Sage

Cranberry Pickled Pumpkin

Lemon-Spiked Basmati Rice

Toasted Garlic & Ginger
Soy-Glazed Bok Choy

Wasabi Mashed Potatoes

Wild Mushroom Risotto

Sweet & Sour Ruby Cabbage

Colorful Jasmine Rice

Brussels Sprouts with Toasted Walnut Butter

Creamy Double-Corn Polenta

Cumin-Grilled Zucchini with
Tomato-Corn Summer Salsa

Balsamic Braised Greens

Blue Cheese Scalloped Potatoes

Confetti Garlic Mashed Potatoes

Ultimate Mom's Turkey Stuffing for a Crowd

DON'T USE THIN ASPARAGUS FOR THIS RECIPE—LOOK FOR FAT, TENDER SPEARS THAT ARE IN SEASON—THEY ARE TASTIER AND GRILL BETTER.

• • •

GRILLED ASPARAGUS
WITH HAZELNUT AIOLI

2 bunches (about 2 pounds) fat asparagus

Olive oil for brushing asparagus

Salt

Hazelnut Aioli (recipe follows)

Wash the asparagus and trim off the bottom 3 inches. Meanwhile, prepare a very hot grill.

Lightly brush asparagus with olive oil. Grill for about 1 minute on each side, until the spears have nice grill marks and are just barely tender. Sprinkle with a little salt.

Serve hot, warm, or even cold. Drizzle with Hazelnut Aioli or put the aioli in individual dishes for dipping.

Makes 1½ cups

• • •

HAZELNUT AIOLI

½ cup toasted hazelnuts (page 25)

¼ teaspoon sugar

1 tablespoon minced garlic

1½ tablespoons fresh lemon juice

½ teaspoon Dijon mustard

2 egg yolks

½ teaspoon salt

¾ cup light olive oil

¼ cup hazelnut oil

1 tablespoon water

In a food processor, place the hazelnuts, sugar, garlic, lemon juice, mustard, egg yolks, and salt. Process until smooth. In a measuring cup, mix together the olive and hazelnut oils. With the food processor running, SLOWLY drizzle in the oils; the drizzle should be about the width of a spaghetti strand. The mixture will slowly begin to emulsify, forming a mayonnaise-like consistency. (Don't add the oil too fast, or the mixture will break!) When all the oil has been added, pulse in the water. Store, refrigerated, until ready to use. The aioli can be made up to 3 days in advance.

Makes 10 to 12 servings

LAST HOLIDAY SEASON I HAD A BRAINSTORM TO TRY MAPLE SYRUP IN A SCALLOPED SWEET POTATO DISH. WELL, MY EXPERIMENT WAS A HIT! FLAVOR-WISE, IT IS REALLY IMPORTANT TO USE REAL MAPLE SYRUP IN THIS RECIPE. IMITATION SYRUPS WON'T GIVE THE SAME TRUE "ROUNDED" FLAVOR.

MAPLE SCALLOPED SWEET POTATOES WITH SAGE

8 cups (2½ to 3 pounds) peeled and thinly sliced (¼-inch) sweet potatoes

MAPLE CREAM

3 cups cream

½ cup real maple syrup

¼ teaspoon ground nutmeg

2 teaspoons minced fresh thyme

1½ teaspoons finely chopped fresh sage leaves

1½ teaspoons salt

¼ teaspoon black pepper

TOPPING

½ cup dry bread crumbs

3 tablespoons grated high-quality Parmesan

2 teaspoons minced fresh thyme

1 tablespoon minced parsley

2 teaspoons finely chopped fresh sage leaves

Fresh sage leaves for garnish

Preheat the oven to 350°F.

Spray a 3-quart baking dish with nonstick vegetable spray or lightly butter it. Arrange the sliced sweet potatoes in the dish in an even layer. In a large bowl, whisk together the Maple Cream ingredients until well combined. Pour the mixture over the sweet potatoes, and push them down a bit to be sure they are coated in liquid.

In a small bowl, combine the Topping ingredients and set aside.

Bake the potatoes for 35 minutes, and then sprinkle them with the topping. Bake for another 25 to 35 minutes, or until the topping is browned, the potatoes are tender, and the liquid is thickened.

Garnish with a sprinkle of fresh sage leaves.

Makes 2½ cups PICKLE FANATIC THAT I AM, I HAD TO TRY MY HAND AT PICKLED PUMP-
KIN. THIS VERY PRETTY CONDIMENT IS ESPECIALLY YUMMY PAIRED WITH
FAT SANDWICHES OF SMOKED TURKEY OR HAM. WHEN PLACED IN
ATTRACTIVE LITTLE JARS, LABELED, AND TIED WITH SOME FESTIVE RIB-
BON, IT MAKES A NICE TAKE-HOME GIFT FOR GUESTS. TELL THE RECIPI-
ENTS TO KEEP THE PICKLES REFRIGERATED.

• • •

CRANBERRY PICKLED PUMPKIN

**1 cup distilled
white vinegar**

1 cup water

1 cup sugar

**2 teaspoons
chopped ginger**

5 cloves

**1 teaspoon black
peppercorns**

1 cinnamon stick

**2 cups (1-inch dice) peeled
fresh pumpkin**

½ cup cranberries

In a medium stainless steel or glass saucepan, combine the vinegar,
water, sugar, ginger, cloves, peppercorns, and cinnamon stick. Place
over medium-high heat and bring to a low boil.

Add the pumpkin and bring back to a low boil or fast simmer, adjusting the heat as necessary. Cook for about 4 minutes, or until the
pumpkin is just tender. Add the cranberries and cook for 1 more
minute.

Remove from the heat and cool to room temperature. Place the mixture in a noncorrosive container such as a glass jar. Cover and refrigerate until ready to serve. The pickles will keep for up to 3 weeks,
refrigerated.

CHEF'S TIPS:
*When cooking pickled items, it is important to use a
noncorrosive pan such as one made of stainless steel. This ensures
that there is no reaction between the metal and the vinegar.*

LEMON-SPIKED BASMATI RICE IS A TERRIFIC VEGETARIAN ACCOMPANI-
MENT TO CURRIED VEGETABLES. THIS AROMATIC DISH IS ALSO SUPERB
WHEN PAIRED WITH FISH, SCALLOPS, PRAWNS, OR LAMB. IT GETS ITS
ZING FROM BOTH LEMON JUICE AND ZEST. I ALSO LOVE THIS WITH
LIME REPLACING THE LEMON IN THE JUICE AND ZEST.

• • •

LEMON-SPIKED BASMATI RICE

**1 cup basmati rice, rinsed
and well drained**

3 tablespoons butter

**¾ cup (¼-inch
dice) onion**

**1½ teaspoons
minced garlic**

Small pinch cayenne

1½ cups water

**1 tablespoon fresh
lemon (or lime) juice**

**1½ teaspoons minced
lemon (or lime) zest**

2 tablespoons cream

1¼ teaspoons salt

**2 tablespoons
thinly sliced chives**

Preheat the oven to 375°F. Place the very well-drained rice in a
1½-quart baking dish.

Melt the butter in a nonstick or heavy saucepan. Add the onion and
sauté over medium heat until soft, about 2 minutes. Add the garlic
and cook for about 30 seconds. Add the cayenne, water, lemon juice,
lemon zest, cream, and salt, and bring to a boil.

Stir the mixture into the rice, being sure to scrape up and include all
the goodies. Seal tightly with foil and bake for 20 to 25 minutes, or
until the rice is tender and all the liquid is absorbed. Fluff with a fork
before serving, then fold in the chives.

CHEF'S TIPS:
*For basmati rice that's scrumptious and lighter on
the pocketbook, purchase your rice in large quantity in a
burlap bag at a local Indian market.*

Makes 4 to 6 servings BABY BOK CHOY IS FLASH-SAUTÉED IN THIS QUICK AND FLAVORFUL PREPARATION. TOASTING THE GARLIC SLIGHTLY GIVES IT A NUTTY AND RICH FLAVOR.

• • •

TOASTED GARLIC & GINGER SOY-GLAZED BOK CHOY

6 medium-sized baby bok choy, cut in half lengthwise (if on the large side, cut into quarters)

1 tablespoon Asian-style sesame oil

4 cloves garlic, VERY thinly sliced

1 teaspoon chopped ginger

⅛ teaspoon dried red pepper flakes

1 tablespoon soy sauce

1 tablespoon water or chicken stock

2 tablespoons butter, cold, cut into small chunks

Toasted mixed black and white sesame seeds for garnish, optional

Carefully wash the bok choy, keeping the half-heads intact.

In a 12-inch nonstick skillet, heat the sesame oil over medium-high heat until hot. Add the garlic slices, ginger, and red pepper flakes, and sauté for 30 seconds or until toasted, stirring often and taking care not to scorch the garlic.

Add the bok choy and sauté, uncovered, turning the pieces over and stirring occasionally until wilted, about 2 minutes. Add the soy sauce and water or stock, and cover the pan with a tight-fitting lid if the bok choy is still a bit too crunchy. Cook for 1 minute, or until the greens are tender.

Add the butter and stir until it melts and coats the bok choy.

Serve immediately, sprinkled with sesame seeds if desired.

CHEF'S TIPS:

● *Very small baby bok choy can be left whole. Slightly larger ones can be cut in halves or quarters lengthwise. If the baby bok choy are even larger, you can separate the heads, pull off the individual "leaves," and sauté them for a different look. If baby bok choy is not available, you can cut large, full-sized bok choy into 2-inch pieces.*

● *To get very thin slices of garlic, shave each peeled clove on the blade side of a cheese grater.*

MASHED POTATOES ARE A COMFORT FOOD CLASSIC, SO GOOD YOU COULD JUST HAVE A BOWL OF THEM AND A BIG GLASS OF RED WINE FOR DINNER. DON'T THINK IT HASN'T BEEN DONE BEFORE! THIS ASIAN-INSPIRED VERSION IS EXCELLENT SERVED WITH SEARED OR GRILLED SEA BASS, SHRIMP, OR RARE TUNA.

• • •

WASABI MASHED POTATOES

2 to 3 teaspoons wasabi powder, depending upon the heat you like

1 tablespoon water

¾ teaspoon salt, or to taste

2½ pounds (about 3 very large) russet potatoes, peeled and cut in half

Pinch of salt

½ cup milk or half-and-half

6 tablespoons butter

1 tablespoon soy sauce

Chopped fresh cilantro or parsley for garnish, optional

In a very small bowl, mix together the wasabi powder, water, and salt and set aside.

Place the potatoes in a very large pot and cover with water by at least 3 inches. Add a pinch of salt. Bring to a boil, reduce the heat, and cook the potatoes on a low boil until fork-tender, 20 to 30 minutes. Test the potatoes to be sure they're tender all the way through.

Meanwhile, combine the milk or half-and-half, butter, and soy sauce in a small pan. Heat over low heat until the butter is melted and the milk is warm. Remove from the heat and stir in the wasabi mixture. Keep warm.

When the potatoes are cooked, drain them well in a large colander, then return them to the pot. Shake the pot over low heat for about 30 seconds to dry out any remaining water. Reheat the wasabi-butter mixture until hot. Remove the potatoes from the heat and add half of the hot wasabi mixture. (Both the potatoes and the liquid must be hot.) With a heavy-duty whisk or masher, mash the potatoes. Then add the remaining liquid and whip or mash the potatoes until they are fluffy.

Mound the potatoes in a large, warm bowl. Sprinkle with chopped cilantro or parsley, if desired.

CHEF'S TIPS:

Be sure to use fresh wasabi powder. If after you make the potatoes you would like them a bit hotter, just mix a little more wasabi powder with some water to make a runny paste, then stir it in.

LIKE THE ROASTED VEGETABLE RISOTTO ON PAGE 116, THIS RECIPE USES A RISOTTO BASE THAT'S MADE IN ADVANCE. THIS METHOD MAKES IT MUCH MORE REALISTIC TO SERVE RISOTTO—WHICH EVERY-ONE LOVES!—WHEN ENTERTAINING BECAUSE YOU'RE NOT TIED TO THE STOVE FOR SO LONG. ONCE YOU'VE TRIED THIS TECHNIQUE, YOU COULD MAKE IT WITH MANY VARIATIONS, SUCH AS ADDING ROASTED VEGETABLES OR COOKED PRAWNS OR CHICKEN.

• • •

WILD MUSHROOM RISOTTO

3 tablespoons extra virgin olive oil

3 cups thickly sliced or torn fresh wild mushrooms, brushed and picked clean (either use one variety such as chanterelles or morels, or a combination of wild and not so wild mushrooms)

¼ cup dry white wine

1¾ cups chicken stock, more or less as needed

Risotto Base (recipe follows)

2 teaspoons minced fresh thyme

4 tablespoons (½ stick) butter, cut into small pieces

½ cup high-quality grated Parmesan

Salt and black pepper

GARNISHES

Grated high-quality Parmesan

Fresh herb sprigs, optional

In a wide, heavy saucepan, Dutch oven, or skillet, heat the olive oil over medium-high heat and add the mushrooms. Sauté for 4 to 5 minutes, or until soft.

Add the white wine and stock, and bring to a boil. Immediately stir in the Risotto Base. Stirring often, let the mixture reduce to a creamy but still brothy consistency, about 5 minutes. The risotto should be heated through at this point. If it gets too thick, add a little water.

Turn off the heat and immediately stir in the thyme, butter, and Parmesan. Taste the risotto and season as needed with salt and black pepper.

Divide the risotto among warm bowls and sprinkle with a little grated Parmesan. Garnish with fresh herb sprigs, if desired.

For a lighter or vegetarian version: Decrease the butter to 2 table-spoons and the Parmesan to ¼ cup. Make the Wild Mushroom Risotto and Risotto Base with vegetable or mushroom broth.

● ● ●

RISOTTO BASE

3 cups homemade chicken stock, lightly salted (or 2 cups canned broth plus 1 cup water)

1 tablespoon olive oil

¾ cup chopped button or chanterelle mushrooms

2 teaspoons minced garlic

1 tablespoon minced shallots

1½ cups arborio rice

¾ cup dry white wine

In a pan, heat the chicken stock (or canned broth plus water) until it comes to a simmer. Lower the heat and keep the stock warm; do not boil or reduce it.

Heat the olive oil over medium-high heat in a wide, heavy saucepan. When the oil is hot, add the mushrooms and sauté lightly, about 2 minutes.

Add the garlic, shallots, and rice. Cook for about 1 minute, stirring continuously. Reduce the heat to medium and add the white wine. Cook until the wine is almost totally absorbed, stirring often, 1 to 1½ minutes.

Stir in one-third of the warm stock. Simmer slowly, stirring often and adjusting the heat if necessary. Cook until the liquid is almost totally absorbed, about 6 minutes.

Stir in another third of the broth. Simmer slowly, stirring often, until the liquid is almost completely absorbed, 6 to 8 minutes. Repeat with the last third of the broth.

The rice should now be a bit creamy in consistency but al dente (firm to the bite) in the center. Immediately remove the pan of rice from the heat and spread the rice out on a rimmed cookie sheet or baking pan. Let cool at room temperature for 15 to 20 minutes. When completely cooled, place in a container with a tight-fitting lid and refrigerate until needed, up to 3 days.

CHEF'S TIPS:
- *Don't wash wild mushrooms, but brush or wipe off any dirt with a pastry brush. Scrape or trim off any bad spots or woody end parts.*
- *Store any mushrooms, refrigerated, in a PAPER BAG—not a plastic bag (they sweat in there)—for up to a week if they are very fresh.*

Makes 8 to 12 servings   I LOVE THE TANGY FLAVORS OF DRIED CRANBERRIES AND GRANNY
SMITH APPLES IN THIS EVER SO-SEASONAL VEGETABLE SIDE DISH.

• • •

SWEET & SOUR RUBY CABBAGE

**6 tablespoons
dried cranberries**

**2 tablespoons
cranberry juice**

¼ cup red wine vinegar

¼ cup currant jelly

**Pinch dried red
pepper flakes**

**¼ cup packed
brown sugar**

**1½ teaspoons ground
coriander**

1 tablespoon cornstarch

**2 tablespoons
butter or olive oil**

**2 large Granny Smith
apples, unpeeled, cored and
cut into ¾-inch dice**

**1 large onion, cut
into ¾-inch dice**

**6 cups packed, cored, and
sliced (¼-inch) red cabbage**

1 teaspoon salt

¼ teaspoon black pepper

In a bowl, whisk together the dried cranberries, cranberry juice, vinegar, currant jelly, red pepper flakes, brown sugar, coriander, and cornstarch. Let sit for 10 minutes.

In a large Dutch oven or skillet, heat the butter or olive oil over
medium-high heat. Add the apples and onion and cook, stirring
often, for about 4 minutes, or until lightly browned.

Add the cabbage and cook, stirring often, for 4 to 5 minutes, or until
the cabbage is wilted.

Whisk the reserved cranberry juice mixture well, making sure any
cornstarch that had settled to the bottom is well incorporated. Add
this mixture to the cabbage and stir well. Cook for about 2 minutes,
until the mixture is thickened and the cabbage is well glazed. Stir in
the salt and pepper.

CHEF'S TIPS:
*This recipe is almost better if it's prepared a day or two
ahead so that the flavors have time to marry. Reheat it BRIEFLY OVER
HIGH HEAT in a skillet so the cabbage retains its crunchy texture.*

Makes 8 to 12 servings

WHEN YOU COOK JASMINE RICE, IT FILLS YOUR HOUSE WITH ITS WONDERFUL SCENT. FRESH LEMONGRASS AND KAFFIR LIME LEAVES CAN BE FOUND AT SOUTHEAST ASIAN GROCERS. IF PURCHASING A PACKAGE OF FRESH LIME LEAVES, USE WHAT YOU NEED AND STORE THE REST IN THE FREEZER. IF FRESH OR FROZEN KAFFIR LIME LEAVES ARE NOT AVAILABLE, TRY TO FIND THEM DRIED.

• • •

COLORFUL JASMINE RICE

RICE

2 cups jasmine rice

3 cups water

¼ cup diced red onion

1½ teaspoons minced ginger

1 teaspoon minced garlic

1¼ teaspoons salt

1½ teaspoons finely minced fresh lemongrass

1 fresh or frozen kaffir lime leaf

CONFETTI

2 tablespoons very finely minced carrot

2 tablespoons very finely minced red bell pepper

3 tablespoons very thinly sliced green onion

To cook in a rice cooker: Rinse the rice in a strainer until the water runs clear. Shake the rice and drain well. Place the rice in a rice cooker with the remaining rice ingredients. Stir well, cover, and steam until tender, following the manufacturer's directions. After the rice is cooked, fluff it with a fork and gently fold in the confetti ingredients.

To cook without a rice cooker: Preheat the oven to 400°F. Rinse the rice in a strainer until the water runs clear. Shake the rice and drain well. Place the rice in a large, ovenproof saucepan with the remaining rice ingredients. Place the pan over high heat and bring to a boil. Stir, then quickly cover the pan with a piece of foil and a tight-fitting lid. Place the pan in the oven and cook for 15 minutes. After the rice is cooked, immediately remove the lid and foil. Fluff the rice with a fork and gently fold in the confetti ingredients.

Serve immediately.

CHEF'S TIPS:

Leftover jasmine rice makes great fried rice. Quickly sauté some veggies and a little leftover meat or chicken in a little oil with the leftover rice. Whisk a little soy sauce with an egg or two and stir-fry it into the rice. Cook until the egg just coats the rice.

LET'S CHAT ABOUT BRUSSELS SPROUTS. FOR YEARS I COULDN'T EVEN BEAR THE THOUGHT OF THEM—REMEMBERING THEM ONLY AS STINKY, OVERCOOKED LITTLE CABBAGES. BUT AFTER A LOT OF BRUSSELS-SPROUTS-CORRECTLY-COOKED "THERAPY," I WILL HAPPILY EAT THOSE *PETITES CHOUX*, ESPECIALLY WHEN LIGHTLY STEAMED AND SLATHERED WITH TOASTED WALNUT BUTTER. . . . STINKY CABBAGES, BEGONE!

· · ·

BRUSSELS SPROUTS WITH TOASTED WALNUT BUTTER

¾ cup walnut pieces

4 tablespoons (½ stick) butter

¾ teaspoon salt

¼ teaspoon black pepper

1 tablespoon fresh lemon juice

1½ teaspoons minced lemon zest

2 tablespoons real maple syrup

6 cups (about 3 pounds) trimmed and halved fresh Brussels sprouts

Preheat the oven to 350°F.

Spread the walnuts on a baking pan and place in the preheated oven for about 5 minutes, or until the nuts are lightly toasted and golden. Let cool.

Place the butter, salt, pepper, lemon juice, zest, and maple syrup in a food processor and process until smooth. Add the cooled walnuts, and pulse until the butter mixture is almost smooth but small pieces of walnut are still visible.

Steam the Brussels sprouts in a steaming basket over boiling water until just tender but not overcooked. Immediately toss with the softened walnut butter and serve.

CHEF'S TIPS:

● If making the walnut butter ahead of time, it can be refrigerated for up to 1 week or frozen for up to 1 month. Be sure to bring it to room temperature before using.

● Another way to serve the Brussels sprouts is to peel each "leaf" off and sauté the leaves in the walnut butter.

THIS CREAMY-STYLE POLENTA GETS A DOUBLE CORN KICK WITH THE ADDITION OF CORN KERNELS.

• • •

CREAMY DOUBLE-CORN POLENTA

1 cup fresh or frozen corn kernels

2 to 4 tablespoons butter

½ cup (¼-inch dice) yellow or white onion

1 small red bell pepper, cut into ¼-inch dice, optional

2 teaspoons minced fresh rosemary

1½ teaspoons minced lemon zest

1 teaspoon minced garlic

2 cups chicken stock

1 cup polenta

3 cups water

1 teaspoon salt

¼ cup grated high-quality Parmesan

Coarsely chop the corn or process it in a food processor until chopped into ⅛- to ¹⁄₁₆-inch pieces. Set aside.

In a large, heavy saucepan over medium-high heat, melt 2 tablespoons butter. Sauté the onion and red pepper for 1½ minutes. Add the rosemary, lemon zest, and garlic, and sauté for 30 seconds more.

Stir in the stock, polenta, water, salt, and reserved corn, and bring to a boil. Reduce the heat to medium and simmer the polenta, stirring occasionally, for 12 minutes, or until thick and thoroughly cooked. As the polenta begins to thicken, stir it constantly.

Stir in the Parmesan and the remaining 2 tablespoons butter, cut into small chunks, if desired.

Serve immediately.

For a lighter version: Replace the butter with 2 tablespoons olive oil when sautéing the vegetables and omit the additional butter at the end.

CHEF'S TIPS:

Try to purchase "coarse" polenta for its pleasing texture. When cooking polenta, you want to make sure that it gets cooked through completely. Be sure to stir it constantly once it has thickened and is in the last stages of cooking.

THESE CAN BE SERVED HOT OR AT ROOM TEMPERATURE. IT'S A GREAT
DISH TO TAKE TO A SUMMER BARBECUE OR PICNIC POTLUCK.

• • •

CUMIN-GRILLED ZUCCHINI WITH TOMATO-CORN SUMMER SALSA

SALSA

¾ cup (¼-inch dice) ripe tomatoes

1 cup (about 1 ear) fresh, sweet corn kernels

¼ cup finely diced red onion

1 fresh jalapeño, seeded and minced

1 tablespoon red wine vinegar

2 tablespoons olive oil

2 tablespoons chopped fresh cilantro

¾ teaspoon salt

¼ teaspoon ground cumin

•

1 tablespoon olive oil

1 teaspoon ground cumin

½ teaspoon salt

¼ teaspoon black pepper

3 medium (about 1¼ pounds) zucchini

Sour cream

To make the Tomato-Corn Summer Salsa: In a large bowl, mix all of the ingredients together well. Some jalapeños are hotter than others, so try a little piece before mixing it all in, then adjust the amount of jalapeño as needed for the desired spiciness.

Get the coals going for a very hot grill.

In a large bowl, mix together the olive oil, cumin, salt, and pepper. Cut each zucchini in half lengthwise and add to bowl. Rub the oil mixture over the zucchini, making sure they are coated well.

Place the zucchini over very hot coals and grill for 2 to 3 minutes on each side to mark the zucchini nicely. Cook until just done. Depending on how hot the grill is and how done you like your vegetables, the total cooking time can vary from 4 to 10 minutes.

Serve the zucchini topped with Tomato-Corn Summer Salsa and a dollop or squiggle of sour cream.

CHEF'S TIPS:
Because the corn in the salsa is not cooked, you will want to use the freshest of summer corn for its tender and sweet character.

BRAISED GREENS ARE THE PERFECT ACCOMPANIMENT TO JUST ABOUT ANYTHING. I LOVE THEM WITH A SIMPLE GRILLED STEAK OR A LEMON-AND-GARLIC-STUFFED ROAST CHICKEN. IF YOU'VE NEVER COOKED GREENS BEFORE, DON'T LET THE SHEER VOLUME OF THE RAW GREENS SCARE YOU OFF. THEY WILL WILT DOWN IN NO TIME.

• • •

BALSAMIC BRAISED GREENS

1½ tablespoons balsamic vinegar

2 tablespoons chicken or vegetable stock

½ teaspoon salt

2 teaspoons cornstarch

2 tablespoons olive oil

½ cup (¼-inch dice) onion

¼ teaspoon dried red pepper flakes

2 teaspoons minced garlic

3 bunches assorted hearty greens, such as green kale, red or Swiss chard, turnip greens, and escarole, washed and cut into 4-inch pieces

In a small cup, mix together the balsamic vinegar, stock, salt, and cornstarch. Set aside.

In a very large stainless steel Dutch oven or heavy soup pot, heat the oil over medium-high heat until it just becomes hot. Add the diced onion and red pepper flakes. Cook for about 2 minutes, stirring often. Add the garlic and washed greens, stir well, and cover.

Cook for 2 minutes, then uncover and stir again. Cover and cook for an additional 2 minutes. Stir the reserved vinegar mixture well, making sure the cornstarch is incorporated, and drizzle it into the pan. Stir, coating the greens well. Increase the heat to high and cook for 1 to 2 minutes more, stirring the greens often, until the broth is slightly thickened and the greens are tender and wilted.

CHEF'S TIPS:

● *"Baby" braising greens mixes are often available in gourmet markets. I love them for their combination of great greens and ease of preparation.*

● *In place of olive oil, you can use bacon fat or pancetta fat to sauté the onions. Just cook up some chopped pancetta or bacon in the pan until half done before adding the onions. Then proceed with the recipe.*

THE PERFECT POTATO DISH FOR A LARGE PARTY! THIS ROBUST VER-
SION OF SCALLOPED POTATOES GETS A KICK FROM BLUE CHEESE,
FRESH THYME, AND ROSEMARY.

• • •

BLUE CHEESE SCALLOPED POTATOES

5 pounds russet potatoes

3 teaspoons salt

½ teaspoon black pepper

**1 teaspoon
minced fresh thyme**

**1 teaspoon
minced fresh rosemary**

**¾ cup (3 ounces)
crumbled blue cheese**

¾ cup grated Parmesan

1 cup sour cream

2 cups cream

Preheat the oven to 350°F. Butter a 9- by 13-inch glass baking dish.

Peel and slice the potatoes ¼-inch thick. Toss them in a large bowl with 2
teaspoons of the salt and the pepper, thyme, and rosemary. In a small
bowl, toss together the cheeses.

Layer half the potatoes in the buttered baking dish. Sprinkle with half
the cheese mixture and top with the remaining potatoes.

In a bowl, whisk together the sour cream, cream, and remaining
1 teaspoon salt and pour over the potatoes. Tap the baking dish on
the counter to spread out the sauce and help release any air bubbles. Sprinkle with the remaining cheese mixture.

Bake the potatoes for about 1 hour and 15 minutes, or until
browned and completely tender all the way through when poked
with a knife. Serve immediately.

You can also make these in advance and store, covered and refrigerated, for up to 2 days. Bring to room temperature and reheat in a
350°F oven until hot.

CHEF'S TIPS:

*Guests are very impressed when I serve these potatoes as individual
round towers. Little do they know how easy it is: Chill the cooked
potatoes totally, then cut them into 12 circles with a deep, 2½-inch round
cutter. Place the potato circles on a parchment-lined baking sheet and
refrigerate until needed. Reheat them in a 400°F oven
until warmed through and nicely browned.*

Makes 6 servings THESE POTATOES HAVE A FUN TWIST: TINY PIECES OF COLORFUL VEG-
GIES, LIGHTLY SAUTÉED AND FOLDED IN FOR TEXTURE AND CRUNCH.
AND THEN, OF COURSE, THERE'S THE GARLIC . . . JUST ENOUGH.

• • •

CONFETTI GARLIC MASHED POTATOES

**2½ pounds russet potatoes,
peeled and cut into halves
or thirds depending on size**

Pinch salt

½ cup milk

Pinch white pepper

**6 tablespoons
(¾ stick) butter**

1 tablespoon minced garlic

¾ teaspoon salt

2 tablespoons sour cream

CONFETTI

½ tablespoon butter

**2 tablespoons very
finely diced carrots**

**2 tablespoons very
finely diced celery**

**2 tablespoons very
finely diced leeks**

**1 tablespoon minced fresh
chives or parsley**

Place the potatoes in a large pot and cover with water. Add a pinch
of salt. Bring to a boil, then reduce the heat and cook on a low boil
until the potatoes are fork-tender, about 20 minutes.

In a small pan, heat the milk, white pepper, butter, garlic, and salt
over low heat until the butter is melted. Do not boil. Remove from
the heat and stir in the sour cream. Keep warm.

To make the confetti: In another small pan, combine the butter with
the carrots, celery, and leeks. Heat over medium heat until just
warmed through and slightly tender.

When the potatoes are cooked, drain them well in a large colander,
then return them to the pot. Shake the pot over low heat for about 30
seconds to dry out any remaining water. Remove from the heat and
add half the hot milk mixture. (Both the potatoes and the liquid must
be hot.) With a heavy-duty whisk or masher, mash the potatoes. Then
add the remaining liquid and whip the potatoes until they are fluffy.

Mix in three-quarters of the confetti vegetables and mound the potatoes in a large, warm bowl. Sprinkle with the remaining vegetables
and the minced chives or parsley.

CHEF'S TIPS:
● *You can easily mulitply this recipe by four to serve a crowd . . . because
you can never have too much mashed potatoes for those family holidays!*
  ● *The most important step in making mashed potatoes is to mash
or whip your potatoes immediately when they are very hot. Cooled
potatoes make a mondo, gluey mess!*

Makes about 32 cups
(two 9- by 13-inch pans, or
stuffing for a very large turkey
and 1 baking dish)

STUFFING IS DEFINITELY A CLOSE RUNNER-UP TO MASHED POTATOES AS A COMFORT FOOD FAVORITE. HOLIDAYS BRING THE "STUFFED BIRD," WHICH USUALLY MEANS ONLY 3 TO 4 CUPS OF STUFFING FOR A CROWD OF 12. AHHHH, I HATE THAT!! WELL, HERE IS A BIG—HUGE— MOM-STYLE STUFFING RECIPE. COPY IT AND HANG IT CONSPICUOUSLY ON YOUR REFRIGERATOR, OR POP IT ANONYMOUSLY IN THE MAIL TO THE RELATIVE WHO DESPERATELY NEEDS THIS PIECE OF CULINARY GUIDANCE.

• • •

ULTIMATE MOM'S TURKEY STUFFING FOR A CROWD

3 gallons (48 cups) firm bread cubes, ½-inch dice

1½ pounds (6 sticks) butter or margarine

About 6 cups (2 very large) diced yellow or white onion

About 5 cups diced celery

4 cups (about ¾ pound) chopped mushrooms

¼ cup finely chopped garlic

4 large eggs

1 bunch parsley, rinsed and finely chopped

1 bunch green onions, thinly sliced

1 cup chopped water chestnuts

1 tablespoon salt

1 teaspoon black pepper

2 tablespoons rubbed dried sage

Let the bread cubes sit out overnight, or lightly dry them out in a warm oven.

Preheat the oven to 350°F.

In a very large pot, melt the butter and sauté the onions, celery, mushrooms, and garlic over medium to medium-high heat. When the vegetables are tender, remove from the heat and let cool.

In a super-mondo mixing bowl, whisk the eggs and mix in the sautéed vegetable and butter mixture, parsley, green onions, water chestnuts, and seasonings. Lightly mix in the bread cubes, then gradually add the stock. You may need more or less stock, depending on how much the bread absorbs; the dressing should be very moist.

Lightly grease one or two 9- by 13-inch baking dishes. Divide the stuffing between the dishes (or use one pan and stuff a turkey).

Loosely cover the baking dish with foil. Bake for 40 to 45 minutes, or until hot in the center. Remove the foil and bake for 10 to 15 minutes more to brown the top.

1 tablespoon dried thyme

2 teaspoons
poultry seasoning

1 teaspoon celery seeds

About 6 cups Rich Turkey
Stock (recipe follows) or
low-sodium canned broth

Makes about 10 cups

● ● ●

RICH TURKEY STOCK

2 large turkey legs or thighs
(about 2 pounds total)

1 yellow onion, unpeeled,
coarsely chopped

1 large or 2 medium carrots,
cut into large chunks

Up to 2 cups mushroom
stems, optional

4 stalks celery, cut into
chunks

½ teaspoon dried thyme

1 bay leaf

½ cup white wine

12 cups water

Preheat the oven to 400°F.

Roast the turkey pieces in a baking pan for 45 minutes to 1 hour, until the skin is golden brown. Place them in an 8-quart pot and add the vegetables and seasonings. Deglaze the roasting pan with the wine, scraping the pan well to loosen the browned bits, and add to the pot. Add the water.

Place the pot over medium-high heat and bring to a rapid simmer. Reduce the heat to low and simmer lightly for 45 minutes to 1 hour. Strain the stock and skim off any fat. Discard the vegetables. (Most of the flavor will have cooked out of the turkey; however, the meat can be removed from the bones and saved for another use.)

CHEF'S TIPS:

● *When stuffing a turkey, do so just before roasting; do not stuff it the night before. Loosely stuff the turkey so that the stuffing will completely cook through. Do not pack the stuffing. You can stuff both ends of a turkey, the large inside cavity and the smaller nook under the skin flap at the neck.*
● *The stuffing in a turkey must come to an internal temperature of 160°F on a thermometer. Before removing the stuffing and carving, let the turkey stand for 15 minutes, allowing the juices to set and the stuffing temperature to rise to 165°F.*

COMFORTS

Classic Meat Loaf with Red Eye
Barbecue Sauce

Chicken, Artichoke & Parmesan Baked Penne

Sunday Slow-Cooked Roast Beef with
Half a Bottle of Wine & 20 Cloves of Garlic

Roast Turkey with Old-Fashioned
Turkey Mushroom Gravy

Pan-Sized Berry Pancakes with Citrus Syrup

Pacific Rim Chicken Pot

Tam's White Heat Mac & Cheese

Chicken & Mushroom Stroganoff
with Parsley Noodles

Slow-Braised Pork Pot Roast
with Apples & Onions

Makes 6 servings, with some leftovers for sandwiches (maybe)

NO LONGER A TREND, THIS MALIGNED DINNER OF THE '60S IS NOW A MAINSTAY. THE MORE TIME-IMPOVERISHED PEOPLE BECOME, THE MORE NEEDY THEY ARE FOR SOME GOOD OL' HOME COOKING THAT'S "JUST LIKE MOM'S." IT TRULY MAKES US STRESSED-OUT OVERACHIEVERS FEEL ALL SQUISHY AND GOOD INSIDE TO DINE ON OLD FOOD-MEMORY FAVORITES.

• • •

CLASSIC MEAT LOAF WITH RED EYE BARBECUE SAUCE

2½ pounds ground beef

3 eggs

1½ tablespoons Worcestershire

¼ cup Heinz 57 Sauce

¼ cup ketchup

½ cup (¼-inch chop) green bell pepper

1 cup (¼-inch chop) yellow onion

½ cup (¼-inch chop) celery

1 tablespoon minced garlic

¼ cup uncooked rolled oats

⅓ cup fine, dry bread crumbs

¾ teaspoon black pepper

2 teaspoons salt

Red Eye Barbecue Sauce (recipe follows)

Bacon slices for garnish, optional

Preheat the oven to 350°F.

Mix all ingredients except the Red Eye Barbecue Sauce and bacon together until well combined. Spray a 9- by 5-inch (8-cup) loaf pan with nonstick vegetable spray. Place the meat mixture in the pan and pack well, being sure to round and smooth the top. Rap the pan on the counter to remove any air bubbles.

Brush the meat with Red Eye Barbecue Sauce (or ketchup). Place bacon slices over the meat, if desired. If not using bacon, cover the meat loaf with foil. Place on a baking sheet and bake for 1 hour. Remove the foil, if used. If you wish, baste the top of the meat loaf with additional sauce or ketchup. Bake 45 to 60 minutes more, or until the meat loaf reaches an internal temperature of 160°F. Cool the meat loaf for 10 minutes, then loosen it from the sides of the pan with a knife. Drain off the grease and unmold the loaf from the pan.

Serve in thick slices, and pass warmed Red Eye Barbecue Sauce on the side.

THE "RED EYE" IN THE NAME COMES FROM ADDED COFFEE, THE KEY INGREDIENT IN TRADITIONAL RED EYE GRAVY MADE FROM THE PAN DRIPPINGS FROM FRIED HAM STEAK DEGLAZED WITH LEFTOVER COFFEE. THIS SAUCE IS ALSO GREAT SLATHERED ON PORK RIBS OR GRILLED STEAK.

Makes 2¼ cups

● ● ●

RED EYE BARBECUE SAUCE

1 tablespoon olive oil

⅓ cup (¼-inch chop) yellow onion

½ teaspoon black pepper

⅛ teaspoon celery seed

¼ teaspoon ground coriander

¼ teaspoon ground cumin

¾ teaspoon dry mustard

1 tablespoon minced garlic

¼ cup apple cider vinegar

½ cup brewed coffee

5 tablespoons Worcestershire

3 tablespoons molasses

⅓ cup packed dark brown sugar

1 cup ketchup

¾ teaspoon Tabasco

1½ teaspoons soy sauce

⅛ teaspoon salt

Heat the oil in a heavy saucepan over medium-high heat. Add the onion and sprinkle the black pepper and other dry spices on top. Stir and sauté until the onions are glossy, about 3 minutes. Add the garlic and continue to sauté for about 1 more minute.

When the onions are translucent, whisk in the remaining ingredients. Bring to a low boil, then reduce the heat and simmer for 30 minutes, stirring frequently to prevent scorching. If not using the sauce right away, cool and store, refrigerated, for up to 10 days.

CHEF'S TIPS:

Most meat loaves can be shaped either by packing the mixture into a loaf pan or ring mold, or by patting it into a free-form oval, round, or rectangle and placing it on a rimmed baking sheet or in a baking dish. The cooking time will vary depending on the shape; a good instant-read thermometer is your best guide. Individual-sized meat loaves, baked in mini-loaf pans or in muffin tins, take only about 30 minutes to bake.

THIS IS A GREAT ENTRÉE TO SERVE TO A CROWD; IT COMBINES POPU-
LAR INGREDIENTS THAT EVERYONE LOVES. YOU CAN ASSEMBLE THIS
DISH A DAY IN ADVANCE AND BAKE IT THE NEXT DAY.

• • •

CHICKEN, ARTICHOKE
& PARMESAN BAKED PENNE

**4 tablespoons (½ stick)
butter or margarine**

2 tablespoons olive oil

**1 pound boneless,
skinless chicken breast,
cut in 1-inch pieces**

1½ teaspoons salt

¼ teaspoon black pepper

**2 cups sliced crimini
mushrooms**

2 tablespoons minced garlic

**1 tablespoon chopped
fresh thyme**

1 teaspoon dried oregano

⅛ teaspoon cayenne

6 tablespoons flour

5 cups milk

1 pound dry penne pasta

**½ cup pitted, chopped
kalamata olives**

**1 (13.75 ounce) can
artichoke hearts, drained
and coarsely chopped**

⅓ cup sliced green onions

**1 cup grated
high-quality Parmesan**

**2 cups (7½ ounces) grated
mozzarella cheese**

Preheat the oven to 375°F. Lightly butter or spray a 9- by 13-inch baking pan or deep baking dish.

In a large, heavy skillet, melt the butter with the olive oil over
medium-high heat. Add the chicken pieces. Season with salt and
pepper and sauté for about 3 minutes, until the chicken turns
opaque. Add the sliced mushrooms and cook for an additional 2
minutes, or until the mushrooms are limp. Add the garlic, herbs, and
cayenne and stir for about 20 seconds; do not let the garlic brown.
Stir in the flour and cook for 1 minute, stirring constantly. Immediately
add the milk, stirring vigorously with a whisk. Bring to a simmer and
whisk occasionally until the sauce is thickened, about 6 to 7 minutes.
Remove from the heat and set aside. The sauce can be made 2 days
ahead. Cool to room temperature, cover, and refrigerate.

Meanwhile, bring a large pot of water to a boil and cook the penne
according to the package directions. Drain well.

In a very large bowl, mix together the pasta and sauce. Fold in the
olives, artichoke hearts, green onions, ¾ cup of the Parmesan, and
the grated mozzarella cheese until well combined. Place the mixture
in the prepared dish.

Sprinkle with the remaining ¼ cup Parmesan, and bake for 25 to 30
minutes, or until the pasta is heated through, the sides are slightly
bubbling, and the top is golden brown.

WOW! THE THICKENED PAN JUICES MAKE THE SEXIEST, TASTIEST
ROAST BEEF GRAVY YOU'LL EVER DRIZZLE OVER MASHED SPUDS!

• • •

SUNDAY SLOW-COOKED ROAST BEEF WITH HALF A BOTTLE OF WINE & 20 CLOVES OF GARLIC

1 (3- to 3½-pound) beef chuck roast

2 tablespoons vegetable oil

1 tablespoon kosher salt

½ teaspoon black pepper

1 large onion, peeled and cut into 8 wedges

1½ cups sliced mushrooms

½ bottle (about 1½ cups) red wine

3 tablespoons flour

20 cloves garlic, peeled

5 sprigs fresh thyme

4 carrots, cut into 1½-inch pieces

4 stalks celery, cut into 1½-inch pieces

1 tablespoon chopped fresh basil, optional

Preheat the oven to 325°F.

With paper towels, pat the roast dry. Heat the oil in a large ovenproof Dutch oven over high heat until hot

Rub the roast with the salt and pepper. Place in the hot pan and sear on all sides until well browned. Remove the meat to a platter. Add the onion wedges and mushrooms to the pan and stir for a few minutes, then tuck the roast back into the pan, pulling the onion and mushroom mixture up from under the roast.

Whisk together the wine and flour until smooth and add to the roasting pan, along with the garlic and thyme. Bring to a simmer, then cover and transfer the pan to the oven.

Roast for about 2 hours. Add the carrots and celery and continue to roast for ½ hour to 1 hour, or until the meat is fork-tender.

Stir the basil into the sauce.

Cut the roast into thick slices or large chunks, depending on your preference, and serve with the sauce drizzled over it.

CHEF'S TIPS:

If the sauce is not thick enough, make a cornstarch slurry using 1 tablespoon cornstarch mixed with 2 tablespoons water. Whisk the slurry into the simmering sauce, a little at a time, until the desired thickness is reached.

COOK UP THE RICH TURKEY STOCK AND MAKE THE GRAVY A COUPLE
OF DAYS AHEAD TO SAVE YOURSELF SOME PRECIOUS HOLIDAY TIME!

ROAST TURKEY WITH OLD-FASHIONED
TURKEY MUSHROOM GRAVY

1 (12- to 18-pound) turkey

Ultimate Mom's Turkey Stuffing (page 148), optional

Herb sprigs and aromatic vegetables such as carrots, celery, onions, and/or leeks, optional

1 tablespoon olive oil

1 to 1½ teaspoons kosher salt

¼ to ½ teaspoon freshly ground black pepper

Old-Fashioned Turkey Mushroom Gravy (recipe follows)

Place an oven rack low in the oven, removing extra racks if necessary. Preheat the oven to 375°F.

Remove the giblets and neck from the turkey cavity. Rinse the turkey with cold water inside and out, and pat dry.

If baking your stuffing in the turkey, see Ultimate Mom's Turkey Stuffing (page 148) for stuffing tips. (The most important thing is not to overstuff the bird! Fill it loosely.) If baking your stuffing separately, place some herb sprigs and chopped aromatic vegetables in the bird's cavity.

Spray a roasting rack with nonstick vegetable spray and place the turkey on the rack in an open, shallow roasting pan. Rub the turkey all over with the olive oil, then sprinkle with the salt and pepper.

Roast the turkey until the inner, thickest part of the thigh registers 175°F. If stuffed, the stuffing must register at least 160°F at the center.

If you are cooking a larger turkey, you may need to tent the breast loosely with a piece of buttered foil to avoid overbrowning. About 30 to 45 minutes before the end of cooking, remove the tent to allow browning.

When the turkey is done, remove it from the oven. Before removing the stuffing and carving the turkey, let it stand for 15 minutes, allowing the juices to settle. The turkey thigh temperature will reach 180°F, and the stuffing temperature will rise to 165°F.

Serve the turkey with Old-Fashioned Turkey Mushroom Gravy.

● ● ●

OLD-FASHIONED TURKEY MUSHROOM GRAVY

**12 tablespoons
(1½ sticks) butter**

**½ teaspoon dried
rosemary, crushed,
or 1 teaspoon minced
fresh rosemary**

**8 ounces (4 cups) thinly
sliced mushrooms**

1 cup flour

**10 cups Rich Turkey Stock
(page 149)**

2 teaspoons salt

½ teaspoon white pepper

Melt the butter in a large, heavy saucepan. Add the rosemary and mushrooms and sauté over medium-high heat for about 2 minutes. Add the flour and stir vigorously until combined and smooth. Cook for about 1 minute. Add the stock all at once and whisk vigorously so as to eliminate any lumps. Reduce the heat and simmer for about 10 minutes, until the gravy is nicely thickened. Season with the salt and white pepper.

CHEF'S TIPS:

*● How large a turkey should you buy? I allow at
least 1½ pounds for each adult, a bit less for children. This assures
leftovers for those all-important midnight turkey sandwiches.*

*● To time the turkey roasting, allow 10 to 15 minutes per
pound, depending on the size of the turkey and
whether it is stuffed. A smaller bird needs more time
per pound; a larger needs less. If stuffed, allow the longer time.
My stuffed, 12-pound turkey took just about 2¾ hours to cook.*

*● While the turkey rests after cooking, you can deglaze
the roasting pan with a little white wine and a tablespoon of brandy.
Scrape up and dissolve all the browned goodies in the pan, then
quickly reduce the liquid over high heat. Add this extra bit
of deliciousness to the gravy you have made ahead
of time while it's reheating.*

THESE ARE LIKE TRADITIONAL PANCAKES MADE WITH LEMON JUICE–SOURED MILK INSTEAD OF BUTTERMILK, PLUS LEMON ZEST FOR A FRAGRANT, TANGY FLAVOR. I'VE LIGHTENED THEM BY FOLDING BEATEN EGG WHITES INTO THE BATTER. EACH ONE IS AS BIG AS A PLATE! TOPPING THEM WITH A DRIZZLE OF HOMEMADE CITRUS SYRUP OR EVEN A LUSH BERRY SYRUP WILL BRING BRIGHT SMILES TO YOUR BREAKFAST TABLE.

• • •

PAN-SIZED BERRY PANCAKES
WITH CITRUS SYRUP

1¾ cups milk

¼ cup fresh lemon juice

2¼ cups flour

2 teaspoons baking powder

½ teaspoon baking soda

3 tablespoons sugar

½ teaspoon salt

1 tablespoon minced lemon zest

2 eggs, separated

4 tablespoons (½ stick) butter, melted

2 cups mixed fresh blueberries and blackberries, or substitute frozen berries

Citrus Syrup, warmed (recipe follows)

Mix the milk and lemon juice together in small bowl and let stand for 10 minutes.

Meanwhile, in a large bowl, mix together the flour, baking powder, baking soda, sugar, salt, and lemon zest.

Whisk the egg yolks into the milk and lemon juice mixture.

Add the liquid mixture all at once to the flour mixture, along with the melted butter, and stir until just incorporated. Do not overmix—some small lumps will remain.

Whip the egg whites until stiff but not dry. Fold half of the egg whites into the batter to lighten it. Then gently fold in the remaining half. Gently fold in the berries.

Preheat a 10-inch nonstick skillet over medium heat. To test the pan, sprinkle with a few drops of water. If they "skittle around," the heat should be just about right.

Ladle 1 cup batter into the pan, being sure to get an even amount of berries for each pancake. If necessary, move the berries around quickly with your fingers to distribute them evenly in the pancake. The pancake should be pan-sized.

Turn the pancake when it is puffed and golden brown and multiple bubbles have appeared. Be sure that the pancake has had enough time to set before turning, since larger pancakes take longer to cook through in the center. Cook on the other side until the pancake is golden and done all the way through. Serve immediately with a drizzle of warmed Citrus Syrup.

Make 1½ cups   • • •

CITRUS SYRUP

1 cup water

2 cups sugar

⅓ cup fresh lemon juice

2 tablespoons lemon zest

In a heavy saucepan, combine the water and sugar and heat over medium heat, stirring to dissolve the sugar. When the sugar is completely dissolved, turn the heat to high. When the syrup comes to a boil, cover the pan and start timing it immediately. Boil the syrup for about 3 minutes.

Uncover and add the lemon juice and zest. Continue boiling, uncovered, for about 3 more minutes, or until the mixture is syrupy. If not using immediately, let it cool to room temperature, then cover and refrigerate. Bring to room temperature or warm slightly before serving.

CHEF'S TIPS:

● *Adjust the heat as needed. When cooking pancakes this large, you need good but slow browning to get the pancakes cooked all the way through in the centers.*

● *If you have an older, more worn nonstick skillet, you may need to oil the pan lightly before using it.*

● *If the Citrus Syrup is too thick when reheating, thin it with a little water. If the syrup is a little too thin, boil for a minute or so to reduce it.*

THIS IS A SLIGHTLY EXOTIC RENDITION OF A HEARTY AND FILLING
CHICKEN SOUP, REINCARNATED INTO A ONE-POT MAIN-DISH MEAL.

• • •

PACIFIC RIM CHICKEN POT

1 (3-pound) whole chicken

**2-inch piece ginger,
unpeeled, sliced ¼-inch**

**1 stalk fresh lemongrass,
split lengthwise, then sliced
in 2-inch pieces**

**5 cloves garlic, unpeeled,
cut in half**

3 quarts cold water

1½ cups ¼-inch sliced celery

2 cups ¼-inch sliced carrots

**1 medium red onion, cut in
⅛- to ¼-inch julienne**

**1 red bell pepper, seeded
and chopped**

2 teaspoons salt

**⅛ to ¼ teaspoon dried red
pepper flakes**

**1 (13- to 14-ounce) can
unsweetened coconut milk**

**Half of a 7-ounce package
thin rice noodles, broken
in half crosswise**

**¼ cup thinly sliced
green onion**

GARNISHES

Chopped fresh cilantro

Lime wedges

Soy sauce

Sliced fresh Thai chiles

Remove any neck pieces or giblets from the chicken cavity. Place the
chicken, ginger, lemongrass, and garlic in a large soup pot. Add the cold
water. Bring to a boil over high heat, then reduce the heat to low and let
simmer, uncovered, until the chicken is tender, about 45 minutes.

Carefully remove the chicken from the pot and refrigerate it in an open
pan to cool it quickly. Strain the stock and discard the seasonings. Let the
stock settle, then skim off the fat. Return the stock to the soup pot and
reduce the liquid over medium-high heat to 6 cups.

When the chicken is cool enough to handle, remove the meat, dis-
carding skin, bone, fat, and cartilage. Cut or tear the chicken meat
into large pieces and reserve.

With the broth at a boil, add the celery, carrots, red onion, bell pepper, salt, and red pepper flakes, and return to a boil. Cook for about
3 minutes, or until the carrots are just tender. Add the coconut milk
and noodles and cook for 2 minutes, or until the noodles are just tender. Add the chicken meat and green onion and heat through, about
2 minutes more.

Divide the "soup goodies" among 6 large bowls, then divide the liquid evenly. Sprinkle each serving with a little chopped cilantro. Pass
the remaining garnishes: limes for squeezing into the soup, soy sauce
for drizzling, and thinly sliced Thai chiles for spiciness.

WHEN GOOFIN' WITH THIS CLASSIC, DON'T FEEL THAT TAKING CRE-
ATIVE LIBERTIES IS SHUNNED. MY GOOD FRIEND AND RESTAURANT
PR DIVA TAMARA WILSON IS A SELF-PROFESSED MAC AND CHEESE
CONNOISSEUR. HER RECIPE FOR WHITE HEAT MAC & CHEESE HAS TO
BE ONE OF THE YUMMIEST YOU'LL EVER EAT—ESPECIALLY IF YOU LIKE
SOME ZIP TO YOUR MAC. YOU CAN USE ALMOST ANY KIND OF SMALL
PASTA SHAPE FOR THIS RECIPE—BOWS, SHELLS, SPIRALS, AND PENNE
ARE GOOD CHOICES. THIS COULD ALSO BE DUBBED THE "OUT TOO
LATE" RESCUE REMEDY.

• • •

TAM'S WHITE HEAT MAC & CHEESE

**4 tablespoons
(½ stick) butter**

1 cup chopped onion

4 teaspoons minced garlic

**1 tablespoon chopped
jalapeños**

**1½ teaspoons
ground coriander**

1½ teaspoons ground cumin

¼ cup flour

4 cups milk

1½ teaspoons salt

**½ cup thick and chunky
medium-hot salsa**

**12 ounces (3 cups)
dry small shell pasta**

**2 cups (about 8 ounces)
grated pepper Jack cheese**

Preheat the oven to 375°F.

In a large, heavy skillet or saucepan, melt the butter over medium
heat. Add the onion, garlic, jalapeños, coriander, and cumin, and
cook, stirring, for about 1 minute. Using a whisk, stir in the flour and
cook for about 1 minute, stirring constantly and vigorously.

Add the milk and continue to whisk until the mixture comes to a simmer,
then stir occasionally until the sauce is thickened, 3 to 4 minutes. Remove
from the heat. Stir in the salt and salsa and set aside.

Meanwhile, bring a large pot of water to a boil and cook the shell pasta
according to the package directions until done. Drain well.

In a very large bowl, mix together the pasta and sauce, then fold in
the Jack and Cheddar cheeses until well combined. Place the mixture in a lightly buttered 9- by 13-inch baking pan.

1½ cups (about 6 ounces) grated white Cheddar cheese

1 cup finely crushed tortilla chips (you can do this in a food processor)

½ cup grated high-quality Parmesan

In a small bowl, mix together the crushed chips and Parmesan, then sprinkle evenly over the top of the mac and cheese.

Bake in the oven for 20 to 30 minutes, or until the pasta is heated through, the sides are slightly bubbling, and the top is golden brown.

CHEF'S TIPS:

I like to use pickled, jarred jalapeños because of their consistent heat. You can certainly use fresh or canned jalapeños, but be sure to take a little taste and adjust the amount to your heat preference.

JUST LOOK AT ALL THE CLASSIC AMERICAN "RETRO" DISHES THAT ARE MAKING SUCH A BIG COMEBACK ON RESTAURANT MENUS. IT'S PRETTY CLEAR THAT DOWN DEEP WE HAVE A SECRET YEARNING FOR YESTER-YEAR DISHES LIKE BEEF STROGANOFF. I'VE TAKEN THAT FAVORITE, REPLACED THE BEEF WITH CHICKEN BREAST, AND WHIPPED UP A SEXY NEW STROGANOFF FOR MODERN TIMES.

• • •

CHICKEN & MUSHROOM STROGANOFF WITH PARSLEY NOODLES

PARSLEY BUTTER

4 tablespoons (½ stick) butter, softened

1 teaspoon minced garlic

¼ cup minced parsley

½ teaspoon salt

2 tablespoons sour cream

CHICKEN

3 tablespoons olive oil

1¼ pounds boneless, skinless chicken breast, cut in about ½-inch by 2-inch strips

¾ teaspoon salt

¼ teaspoon black pepper

1 cup thinly sliced red onion

1½ cups sliced mushrooms

¾ cup high-quality red wine

1½ teaspoons Worcestershire

Place a pot of water on the stove and bring to a simmer. Cover until ready to cook the noodles.

To make the Parsley Butter: In a food processor, combine the butter, garlic, parsley, salt, and sour cream. Process until smooth, then set aside.

To cook the chicken: In a very large nonstick pan, heat 2 tablespoons of the olive oil over medium-high heat until hot. Add the chicken and sprinkle with the salt and pepper. Sauté for 4 to 5 minutes, until the chicken is lightly browned on the outside and about three-quarters cooked. With a slotted spoon, remove the chicken from the pan to a plate and set aside, keeping the pan on the heat.

Add the remaining 1 tablespoon oil to the pan, then add the onion and mushrooms. Stirring often, cook for 2 to 4 minutes, until the onions are tender. Add the wine, turn the heat up to high, and cook until the wine is almost totally evaporated, 4 to 6 minutes.

Meanwhile, in a small bowl, mix together the Worcestershire, beef stock, and cornstarch until smooth. Add the mixture to the pan after the wine has evaporated, and bring to a boil. The sauce should thicken slightly.

(continued)

1 cup beef stock

2 teaspoons cornstarch

¾ cup sour cream

**12 ounces dry wide
egg noodles**

GARNISHES

Sour cream

Italian parsley sprigs

Stir in the ¾ cup of sour cream, then add the reserved chicken. Cook until heated through.

Meanwhile, cook the noodles according to the package directions until just tender. Drain well and place back in the cooking pot. Add the Parsley Butter and stir until well coated.

Divide the noodles among large individual pasta bowls and top with the chicken and sauce. Garnish each serving with a dollop of sour cream and a parsley sprig.

CHEF'S TIPS:

- *I make this recipe with a purchased beef stock. If using a homemade stock, you will need to add additional salt to taste to the sauce.*
- *You can use chicken stock instead, but the flavor won't be as rich.*

MY FRIENDS GO CRAZY FOR THIS FLAVORFUL DISH, NODDING
APPROVAL WHILE FITTING IN COMPLIMENTS BETWEEN MOUTHFULS
AND SOPPING UP EVERY DRIBBLE OF JUICE WITH THEIR BREAD. IT
MAKES A SUPER WINTER MEAL, ESPECIALLY WHEN SERVED WITH
ROASTED RED POTATOES AND ROOT VEGETABLES SUCH AS TURNIPS,
PARSNIPS, OR RUTABAGAS.

• • •

SLOW-BRAISED PORK POT ROAST
WITH APPLES & ONIONS

**1 (2½-pound) boneless pork
shoulder or butt roast**

2 teaspoons salt

¼ teaspoon black pepper

**2 Gala apples, each
cut into 8 chunks**

**1 large onion, cut
into 16 chunks**

2 large sprigs fresh thyme

6 cloves garlic

**1 teaspoon caraway
seeds, optional**

**⅓ cup raspberry or white
wine vinegar**

3 tablespoons sugar

Preheat the oven to 350°F.

Pat dry the pork roast and sprinkle with the salt and pepper. Place
apples, onion, thyme, and garlic in a small roasting pan and set the
pork roast on top. Sprinkle with the caraway seeds.

Mix together the vinegar and sugar until the sugar is dissolved, then
pour it around the pork.

Place the pork in the oven and roast, uncovered, for 1 hour. Cover
the pan with a tight-fitting lid and continue roasting for about 1½
hours more, until the pork is fork-tender. The total roasting time will
be about 2½ hours.

CHEF'S TIPS:
*Gala apples are used in this recipe for their superior,
firm texture when cooking. If Gala apples are not available, try
to find Fujis, which also work well.*

SWEETS

Tropical Fruit Shortcake with Coconut Cream

Frozen "Lemon Drop" Ice Topped with
a Lemon Cream Cloud

Unbelievable Apple Cake with Cider Crème
Anglaise & Cranberry Compote

Fresh Berries with Fluffy Vin Santo
Zabaglione & Hazelnut Biscotti

Oozy Chocolate Grand Marnier Cakes with
Glazed Blood Oranges

Cherries Jubilee Parfaits

Billowing Strawberry Poppy Seed Layer Cake

"Chef-Style" Berry or Fruit Purée

"Gimme Both" Pumpkin-Pecan Pie with
Bourbon Whipped Cream

Flaming Chocolate Praline Alaska

Eggnog Bread Pudding with Rum Caramel

Free-Form Pear & Almond Tarts

Succulent Summer Stone Fruits with
Lavender-Infused Honey Syrup

"Latte Land" Mocha Panna Cottas
with Mocha Sugar Cookies

Cocoa Meringue Straws

COCONUT NUTS, THIS IS FOR YOU! HERE'S A DOUBLE DOSE OF THAT CREAMY, SEDUCTIVE FLAVOR, ALONG WITH PLENTY OF DICED SUNSHINE FROM THE WARMER LATITUDES. I LIKE TO SERVE THIS IN THE WINTER, WHEN TROPICAL FRUITS ARE AT THEIR PEAK AND EVERYONE IS CRAVING A SPLASH OF THE SUN.

• • •

TROPICAL FRUIT SHORTCAKE WITH COCONUT CREAM

1 cup diced ripe pineapple

1 small, ripe mango, peeled and diced

1 small banana, sliced

1 kiwi, peeled and diced

½ cup fresh raspberries or sliced strawberries

2 tablespoons orgeat syrup,* or substitute coconut syrup

2 tablespoons fresh lime juice

1 tablespoon packed brown sugar, more or less to taste

Coconut Cream (recipe follows)

Banana Walnut Cake (recipe follows)

GARNISHES

¼ cup flaked coconut, lightly toasted

6 small pineapple leaves

6 slices star fruit

*Orgeat syrup is an almond-flavored syrup and is available in the flavored syrup or coffee section of well-stocked grocers.

In a large bowl, toss together the prepared fruits, orgeat syrup, lime juice, and brown sugar. Cover and refrigerate.

Just before serving, make the Coconut Cream.

To serve: Trim the crusts from the Banana Walnut Cake (and save for a later snack!). Cut the cake into 6 squares. Place squares of cake on 6 large dessert or dinner plates. Spoon some marinated fruit and some of the juice on top of each square, dividing them equally among the servings. Dollop with the Coconut Cream. If desired, sprinkle the toasted coconut on top, tuck a pineapple leaf under the cake, and stand up a slice of star fruit in the cream.

COCONUT CREAM

¾ cup cream

1 tablespoon packed brown sugar

2 tablespoons Coco Lopez (cream of coconut)

1½ tablespoons dark rum

In a small bowl, whip the cream with the brown sugar until soft peaks form. Lightly whisk in the Coco Lopez and the rum.

BANANA WALNUT CAKE

1 cup flour

1½ teaspoons baking powder

¼ teaspoon salt

4 tablespoons (½ stick) butter, softened

½ cup sugar

½ teaspoon vanilla extract

1 egg

1 large, super-ripe banana, completely brown or at least thoroughly speckled

1 tablespoon fresh lime juice

½ cup walnuts, chopped

Preheat the oven to 350°F. Grease and flour an 8-inch square baking pan.

Sift together the flour, baking powder, and salt. In a mixer, cream the butter and sugar together until light. Add the vanilla and egg and mix until well incorporated.

In a small bowl, mash the banana and lime juice together with a fork. With the mixer running, add the banana mixture and mix until well incorporated. Scrape down the sides.

Add the reserved dry ingredients to the mixer and mix at low speed to incorporate. Add the walnuts and mix well.

Spread the mixture evenly in the prepared baking pan. Bake for 25 to 30 minutes, or until a cake tester or toothpick inserted in the center comes out clean. Remove the cake from the oven and cool in the pan for 10 minutes, then turn the cake out on a rack to cool thoroughly.

PUCKER UP FOR THE ULTIMATE LEMON DESSERT FOR GROWNUPS. THIS IS MY PLAY ON THE EVER-POPULAR LEMON DROP COCKTAIL: FROZEN LEMON ICE LACED WITH VODKA IS SCOOPED INTO OVERSIZED FROZEN MARTINI GLASSES AND TOPPED WITH A "CLOUD" OF CONTRASTING LEMON CREAM.

• • •

FROZEN "LEMON DROP" ICE TOPPED WITH A LEMON CREAM CLOUD

"LEMON DROP" ICE

1¼ cups water

1¼ cups sugar

1 cup fresh lemon juice

6 tablespoons vodka

LEMON CREAM

½ cup cream

6 tablespoons powdered sugar

1 tablespoon fresh lemon juice

1 tablespoon very finely minced lemon zest

•

6 thinly sliced lemon wheels, optional

To make the "Lemon Drop" Ice: In a small pan, bring the water and sugar to a boil over high heat. Let the mixture boil for 30 seconds, then remove it from the heat and cool to room temperature.

Place the cooled mixture in a stainless steel or glass bowl and stir in the lemon juice and vodka. Cover with plastic wrap and place in the freezer. Every half-hour or so, remove the bowl from the freezer and stir the mixture with a fork. It should start becoming slushy after 1½ to 2 hours. When the mixture is icy and completely raked into tiny ice crystals, stop the stirring. Let the mixture freeze overnight, then break up the ice crystals with a fork right before serving.

To make the Lemon Cream: Just before serving, whip the cream, powdered sugar, lemon juice, and zest until the cream forms soft peaks.

Fluff the ice with a fork once more and divide it among 6 frozen oversized martini glasses or dessert dishes. Dollop each serving with the Lemon Cream and garnish with a lemon wheel, if desired.

CHEF'S TIPS:

For a terrific presentation, rim your serving glasses with sugar before freezing them: With a small wedge of lemon, swipe the rim of an oversized (10-ounce) martini glass. Pour about 1 cup of superfine sugar onto a small plate and dip the rim of the glass in the sugar. Repeat with the remaining glasses. Place in the freezer until ready to serve.

CULINARY HISTORIAN AND RESEARCHER JUDY AMSTER GAVE ME THIS RECIPE, TOUTING ITS UNIQUE METHOD AND "INTERESTING" INGREDIENTS—INCLUDING WORCESTERSHIRE! QUITE SIMPLY, THIS IS ONE OF THE BEST CAKES I HAVE EVER MADE!

• • •

UNBELIEVABLE APPLE CAKE WITH CIDER CRÈME ANGLAISE & CRANBERRY COMPOTE

2 cups (about 10 ounces) unpeeled, diced Granny Smith apples

2 cups (about 10 ounces) unpeeled, diced red-skinned apples, such as Braeburn, Winesap, or Jonathan

2 cups sugar

3 cups flour

2 teaspoons baking soda

1 teaspoon salt

2 teaspoons ground cinnamon

1 teaspoon ground allspice

½ teaspoon ground nutmeg

1 cup canola oil

2 eggs, beaten

1 tablespoon Worcestershire

1 cup walnuts, coarsely chopped

½ cup golden raisins

½ cup dark raisins

Cider Crème Anglaise (recipe follows)

Cranberry Compote (recipe follows)

Preheat the oven to 325°F. Grease and flour a 10-inch tube pan or a large Bundt pan and set aside.

Combine the apples and sugar in a large bowl. Let sit for 15 minutes.

Meanwhile, sift the dry ingredients into a bowl. Stir in the oil, eggs, and Worcestershire. Add this mixture to the apple mixture all at once and mix well. Fold in the walnuts and raisins.

Scrape the cake batter into the prepared pan. Rap the pan on the counter to release any bubbles.

Bake for about 1¼ hours, or until a cake tester or toothpick comes out clean when poked into the cake. Cool the cake in the pan, then turn it out onto a cake plate.

To serve: Slice the cake into the desired number of servings. Pool a little Cider Crème Anglaise on individual dessert plates, then place a cake slice on top. Spoon a little Cranberry Compote over each slice. Pass additional Crème Anglaise and Cranberry Compote at the table.

CIDER CRÈME ANGLAISE

In a small bowl, whisk together the egg yolks and sugar until well combined.

4 large egg yolks

¼ cup sugar

1 cup half-and-half

3 tablespoons apple juice concentrate, undiluted

In a double boiler or medium bowl set over a pan of simmering water, heat the half-and-half until hot but not simmering. Whisk half of it into the egg mixture to temper the eggs. Add the tempered egg mixture back into the hot half-and-half, stirring constantly with a whisk. Cook slowly until the sauce just begins to thicken and become slightly shiny, about 5 minutes. (Do not overcook or it will turn into scrambled eggs!)

Immediately remove the bowl from over the hot water. Stir in the apple juice concentrate and place the bowl in another bowl of iced water to cool quickly. Stir often during cooling. Refrigerate until needed, up to 3 days.

CRANBERRY COMPOTE

Place all ingredients in a medium-sized, heavy saucepan over medium-high heat. Bring to a simmer, then reduce the heat to medium. Cook until the cranberries pop and the mixture has a thick compote consistency, 5 to 6 minutes. Let cool completely before serving.

1½ cups fresh or frozen cranberries

¼ teaspoon ground nutmeg

¾ cup sugar

½ cup apple juice

Refrigerate until needed, up to 3 days.

CHEF'S TIPS:

While cranberries are in season, buy a bag and stick them in the freezer. Then, at any time during the year, you can enjoy the cranberry compote. Try it over vanilla ice cream or plain cheesecake for a scrumptious treat!

Makes 6 to 8 servings

MY VERSION OF ZABAGLIONE IS MADE WITH THE SWEET ITALIAN DESSERT WINE, VIN SANTO. ITS CUSTARDY, SWEET TEXTURE IS THEN LIGHTENED WITH WHIPPED CREAM—THE PERFECT FOIL FOR FRESH BERRIES. THIS RECIPE ALSO INCLUDES A TERRIFIC VARIATION MADE WITH FRESH FIGS.

• • •

FRESH BERRIES WITH FLUFFY VIN SANTO ZABAGLIONE & HAZELNUT BISCOTTI

5 egg yolks

5 tablespoons granulated sugar

¾ cup vin santo (Italian dessert wine)

2 pints assorted fresh berries or fresh, ripe figs

1 cup cream

3 tablespoons powdered sugar

Hazelnut Biscotti (recipe follows)

Place the egg yolks, granulated sugar, and vin santo in a large metal bowl. Place the bowl over a pan of simmering water (the bowl must not touch the water). Vigorously whisk with a wire whisk. Cook, whisking continuously, until the mixture is thickened to the consistency of a custard pie filling, about 4 minutes. Remove from the heat and cool to room temperature, whisking occasionally, then refrigerate it for at least 15 minutes, or until slightly chilled.

Meanwhile, clean the berries or figs. Cut up the berries, such as large strawberries, if necessary. If using figs, stem and quarter them. Chill the fruit until ready to serve.

When the egg mixture is totally cool, combine the cream and powdered sugar in a bowl and whip until stiff but not overwhipped.

Add about one-quarter of the whipped cream to the cooled egg mixture and fold it in to lighten the mixture. Then gently fold in the remaining whipped cream until incorporated.

Spoon the zabaglione into small individual dishes. Top each portion with some of the fresh fruit. Serve with Hazelnut Biscotti.

CHEF'S TIPS:
If serving buffet-style, place the zabaglione in a large, chilled, shallow decorative bowl, then top it with the fruit.

HAZELNUT BISCOTTI

1 tablespoon extra virgin olive oil

2 eggs

1 cup sugar

1 teaspoon vanilla extract

1 tablespoon grated orange zest

2½ cups flour

1 teaspoon baking soda

¼ teaspoon salt

¼ teaspoon ground nutmeg

1 cup toasted hazelnuts (page 25), coarsely chopped

2 to 3 teaspoons orange juice, if needed

Preheat the oven to 350°F.

In a small bowl, whisk together the olive oil, eggs, sugar, vanilla, and orange zest until fluffy.

In a large bowl, sift together the flour, baking soda, salt, and nutmeg. Make a well in the center of the dry ingredients, then add the egg mixture and toasted chopped nuts. Mix together until thoroughly combined. (Depending upon where you live and the moisture content in your flour, you may need to add 2 to 3 teaspoons of orange juice if the dough is too dry.)

Spray a baking sheet lightly with nonstick vegetable spray. Roll the dough into a large log and divide it into 4 equal pieces. Roll each piece of dough into another log measuring about 10 inches long by 1 inch in diameter. (If the dough sticks to your work surface, lightly flour the surface.) Place the dough logs, spaced evenly apart, on the baking sheet.

Bake for about 20 minutes, or until baked through and lightly browned.

Remove from the oven and reduce the oven temperature to 250°F. When the cookie logs are cool enough to handle, cut each log into 12 diagonal slices. Place the cookies, a cut side up, on the baking sheet and bake in the oven for 15 to 20 minutes, or until dried out.

Cool on a baking rack, then store at room temperature in a well-sealed container.

EVERYONE LOVES THESE OOZING CHOCOLATE CAKES. IF TIME IS TIGHT, FORGET THE ORANGES AND SERVE THE CAKES WARM, TOPPED WITH A TINY SCOOP OF YOUR FAVORITE VANILLA OR CHOCOLATE ICE CREAM AND A DUSTING OF POWDERED SUGAR.

• • •

OOZY CHOCOLATE GRAND MARNIER CAKES WITH GLAZED BLOOD ORANGES

Glazed Blood Oranges (recipe follows)

6 ounces bittersweet chocolate, chopped into small chunks

10 tablespoons (1 stick plus 2 tablespoons) butter

5 large eggs

½ cup sugar

½ teaspoon vanilla extract

1 tablespoon flour

¼ cup Grand Marnier

Make the Glazed Blood Oranges up to 1 day in advance and chill.

Preheat the oven to 400°F. Spray 6 small glass custard dishes or ramekins very lightly with nonstick vegetable spray and set aside.

To make the cakes: In a double boiler or medium bowl set over a pan of simmering water, combine the chocolate and butter. Heat over medium heat, stirring often, until the butter and chocolate are just barely melted. Remove from the heat and stir until completely melted.

In another bowl, beat together the eggs, sugar, vanilla, flour, and Grand Marnier. Fold in the melted chocolate mixture. Refrigerate batter for 2 hours or overnight.

To serve: Divide the batter evenly among the custard dishes. Place the dishes on a baking sheet and bake for about 18 minutes, or until the cakes are set but the centers are still very, very soft. Let cool for 3 to 4 minutes and serve immediately. Run a knife blade around the rims of each of the custard cups, turn the cakes out onto individual plates top side up, and spoon the Glazed Blood Oranges over and around the cakes.

GLAZED BLOOD ORANGES

3 very large or 4 small blood oranges, or substitute regular oranges

2 tablespoons Grand Marnier or other orange-flavored liqueur, optional

2 tablespoons fresh lemon juice

2 tablespoons water

⅓ cup sugar

Cut a thin slice off the ends of each orange. Holding an orange with a cut end resting on a cutting board, cut the rind off the orange all the way around, using downward cutting motions. Repeat with the remaining oranges. After you have cut away all the rind and white pith from the oranges, cut them into ¼-inch slices and flick out any seeds. Place the orange slices in a large, shallow glass or stainless bowl or baking dish. Sprinkle with the Grand Marnier.

In a small saucepan, combine the lemon juice, water, and sugar. Bring to a boil over high heat and boil for 1 minute. Let cool, then pour the lemon syrup over the sliced oranges. Cover the oranges with plastic wrap and let them marinate, refrigerated, for at least 30 minutes or up to 1 day.

CHEF'S TIPS:
You can make the Oozy Chocolate Grand Marnier Cake batter up to two days in advance and portion into custard cups or a baking dish. Cover with plastic and refrigerate until ready to bake.

OKAY, BIG CONFESSION: I AM *NOT A CHOCOHOLIC, BUT I LOVE* FRUIT DESSERTS! I WAS THE WEIRDO KID WHO, WHEN ASKED WHAT I WANTED FOR MY BIRTHDAY DESSERT, REPLIED, "LEMON MERINGUE PIE" OR "PEACH UPSIDE-DOWN CAKE" OR "CHERRIES JUBILEE"! I GUESS YOU COULD CALL ME A . . . FRUIT HEAD!

• • •

CHERRIES JUBILEE PARFAITS

CHERRY COMPOTE

¾ cup orange juice

¼ cup sugar

1½ tablespoons cornstarch

3 cups pitted, halved cherries

2 tablespoons Grand Marnier or other orange liqueur

To make the Cherry Compote: In a small pan, whisk together the orange juice, sugar, and cornstarch. Place over medium-high heat and bring to a simmer, whisking continuously. Cook until thickened, about 1 minute.

Remove from the heat and fold in the cherries and Grand Marnier. Refrigerate until well chilled, at least 45 minutes. Cherry Compote can be made the day before.

ORANGE CREAM

1 cup cream

6 tablespoons powdered sugar

2 teaspoons minced or grated orange zest

•

5 cups (¾-inch) cubed white cake or pound cake (about one 9-inch cake layer)

⅓ cup slivered almonds, toasted, optional

To make the Orange Cream: Combine the cream, powdered sugar, and orange zest in a large bowl. Using an electric mixer on medium speed, whip the cream until it is just forming peaks. Refrigerate until ready to assemble the parfaits.

To assemble the parfaits: Line up 6 extra-large balloon wine glasses, oversized martini glasses, or dessert parfait glasses. Divide half of the Cherry Compote evenly among the glasses. Then divide half of the cake cubes evenly among the glasses. Spoon half of the Orange Cream evenly onto the cake cubes in each glass. Repeat, ending with Orange Cream on top. Refrigerate for at least 30 minutes before serving. If desired, sprinkle with toasted almonds right before serving.

CHEF'S TIPS:
If the dessert will be part of a serve-yourself buffet table,
assemble it in a large, pretty glass bowl instead of individual glasses.

THIS IS A BEAUTIFUL CAKE TO SERVE FOR A SPECIAL OCCASION, BIRTHDAY, OR SUMMER SOIRÉE. FOR THE ULTIMATE STRAWBERRY SENSATION, SERVE IT ALONGSIDE SCOOPS OF FRESH STRAWBERRY ICE CREAM.

• • •

BILLOWING STRAWBERRY POPPY SEED LAYER CAKE

CAKE

2¼ cups flour

1½ cups sugar

1 tablespoon baking powder

½ teaspoon salt

8 tablespoons (1 stick) butter, softened

1 cup whole milk

2 eggs

1½ teaspoons vanilla extract

2 tablespoons poppy seeds

FROSTING

8 ounces cream cheese, softened

2 teaspoons vanilla extract

3 cups powdered sugar

2 cups cream

(continued)

Preheat the oven to 350°F. Grease and flour three 8-inch round cake pans and set aside.

In the bowl of a standing mixer or other large mixing bowl, sift together the flour, sugar, baking powder, and salt. Add the softened butter. Using an electric mixer, mix on medium speed for 1 minute. Add half of the milk and mix for 2 minutes more to cream the batter. Scrape down the sides of the bowl with a rubber spatula and add the remaining milk, eggs, and vanilla. Continue mixing on medium speed for 2 more minutes. Stir in the poppy seeds.

Divide the batter evenly among the prepared pans and bake for 20 to 25 minutes, or until a cake tester or toothpick inserted in the center comes out clean.

Remove from the oven and cool in the pans on a rack for 10 minutes. Run a knife around the edge of each cake layer and turn it out onto a rack to cool thoroughly.

Meanwhile, make the frosting: Using an electric mixer, beat the softened cream cheese and vanilla on medium speed for 1 minute. Turn the speed to high and mix for 1 minute. Stop the mixer, add 1 cup of the powdered sugar, and mix on low speed for 1 minute. Repeat twice, until all the powdered sugar has been added, then increase the mixer speed to high and whip for 3 minutes.

FILLING

½ cup high-quality strawberry jam

1 pint fresh strawberries, stemmed and thinly sliced

●

1 pint fresh strawberries for garnish

In another bowl, whip the cream until stiff, then fold it gently into the cream cheese mixture until just incorporated. Refrigerate until ready to frost the cake.

To make the filling: In a medium bowl, stir the strawberry jam until smooth, then gently fold in the strawberries. Set aside until ready to fill the cake.

To assemble and frost the cake: On a large cake plate, place 1 layer of the cake. Spoon one-half of the strawberry filling in the center, then spread it out to ¾ inch from the edge. Top with 1 cup of the frosting and spread the frosting to ¾ inch from the edge. Place another layer of cake on top and repeat. Place the final layer of cake on top, then press down gently on the cake layers to stabilize them.

With a large rubber or cake spatula, mound half of the remaining frosting on the top of the cake. Spread the other half around the sides of the cake, covering up all cake and swirling the frosting decoratively. Smooth out the frosting on the top of the cake. Let the frosting dry a little before garnishing the cake.

Stem the garnish berries, and cut them in half lengthwise. Place, cut sides down, around the top edge of the cake. Arrange any extra strawberries in a small pattern in the middle of the cake. Refrigerate the cake until ready to serve.

CHEF'S TIPS:

Bakeries often freeze their cake layers before filling and frosting them, as doing so is easier when the cake is really firm. Generally, by the time you have finished frosting the cake, it has defrosted and is ready to eat.

FRIENDS KEEP ASKING ME HOW TO MAKE THE "CHEF-STYLE FRUIT PURÉES" USED IN RESTAURANT DESSERT PRESENTATIONS. THESE PURÉES ARE ACTUALLY SUPER-EASY. FRUIT PURÉES CAN BE MADE AND STORED IN THE FREEZER IN SMALL BATCHES OR EVEN FROZEN IN SQUIRT BOTTLES. WHEN READY TO USE, SIMPLY PULL A BOTTLE FROM THE FREEZER, DEFROST, SHAKE WELL, AND DECORATE YOUR DESSERT PLATES "CHEF-STYLE."

• • •

"CHEF-STYLE" BERRY OR FRUIT PURÉE

2 cups fresh, ripe berries, such as raspberries or blackberries, or 2 cups unpeeled, sliced ripe peaches or nectarines

¼ cup light corn syrup

1 tablespoon fresh lemon juice

In a blender or food processor, combine all the ingredients and process until very, very smooth. Place a very fine strainer over a bowl. (Be sure your strainer is fine enough so that seeds and skins won't go through.) Transfer the mixture to the strainer. Using the bottom of a ladle or a sturdy spoon, press and stir the purée through the strainer. Use the purée immediately, refrigerate it for up to 1 week, or freeze it for up to 3 months.

CHEF'S TIPS:

● *It is important to use very ripe fruits for this recipe—even overripe fruits are fine.*
● *For decorating desserts, it is nice to use a squeeze bottle and squiggle the purée over the dessert or make cool patterns with it on the plate. Try some dots, circles, or swirls . . .*

Makes 1 (9-inch) pie

THE FAVORITE TRADITIONAL HOLIDAY PIES HAVE GOT TO BE PUMPKIN AND PECAN. HOW MANY TIMES HAVE YOU HEARD, "OOOH, I'LL JUST HAVE A SLIVER OF EACH." I HAVE PUT AN END TO THAT DILEMMA: MY "GIMME BOTH" PIE INCLUDES A LAYER OF PUMPKIN ON THE BOTTOM AND PECAN ON TOP, BAKED INTO PERFECT HARMONY AND TOPPED WITH A POUF OF BOURBON WHIPPED CREAM. YUM!

• • •

"GIMME BOTH" PUMPKIN-PECAN PIE WITH BOURBON WHIPPED CREAM

1 (9-inch) uncooked Classic Flaky Pie Crust (recipe follows)

Preheat the oven to 425°F.

PUMPKIN LAYER

¾ cup canned pumpkin

¼ cup sugar

1 egg

3 tablespoons sour cream

¼ teaspoon ground ginger

½ teaspoon ground cinnamon

⅛ teaspoon ground cloves

⅛ teaspoon ground nutmeg

¼ teaspoon salt

In a medium bowl, whisk together the Pumpkin Layer ingredients. Set aside.

In another bowl, combine all of the Pecan Layer ingredients except the pecans and mix until smooth. Stir in the pecans.

Spread the pumpkin mixture into the unbaked pie shell, then very carefully spoon the pecan mixture over the top, being careful to keep the layers separate. Bake for 15 minutes. Reduce the oven temperature to 350°F and bake the pie for another 25 to 30 minutes, or until the filling is slightly puffy and the pecan layer is just set. Cool on a wire rack.

CHEF'S TIPS:

There are only three things that could be scary about pie-making: (1) You may not be able to control yourself and will end up eating the entire pie. (2) Depending upon how much you get "into it," you could end up having your kitchen looking like a flour bomb exploded. (That is the way mine looks—and it's worth it.) (3) The pie may be so plum full of deliciousness that it will bubble over in your oven, smoke out your house, and set off your fire alarm. A wave of a dish towel and an open door will take care of that . . .

PECAN LAYER

½ cup packed dark
brown sugar

¾ cup dark corn syrup

2 eggs

1 tablespoon butter, melted

1 teaspoon vanilla extract

1 cup pecan halves or pieces

BOURBON
WHIPPED CREAM

1 cup cream

3 tablespoons sour cream

3 tablespoons packed
brown sugar

1 tablespoon bourbon

To make the Bourbon Whipped Cream: In a large bowl, whip the cream, sour cream, and brown sugar until lightly whipped. Stir in the bourbon.

Serve the pie with dollops of Bourbon Whipped Cream. The pie will keep, covered and refrigerated, for 2 to 3 days, but I don't know anyone who could keep this pie that long!

Makes 1 (9-inch) pie crust

• • •

CLASSIC FLAKY PIE CRUST

1 cup flour

¼ teaspoon salt

¼ cup shortening or lard

2 tablespoons cold butter

2 tablespoons ice water

In a large bowl, mix the flour and salt. Cut in the shortening and butter until the particles are pea-sized. Sprinkle in the ice water, 1 tablespoon at a time, mixing gently with a fork until the dough comes together in a ball. Do not over-handle the dough. (If the dough is too soft, press it gently into a disk and refrigerate for about 20 minutes before rolling.) On a lightly floured surface, roll the dough out to a bit bigger than your pan. Brush any excess flour off the dough and fit the dough into the pan. Roll the dough over at the edges, trimming off any excess, then crimp it with your fingers to make a pretty crust edge. Chill the crust until you're ready to fill and bake it.

I LIKE TO MAKE A PETITE ALASKA FOR ROMANTIC DINNERS *À DEUX*, BUT THIS RECIPE ACTUALLY MAKES ENOUGH FOR 4. IF YOU ARE SERVING MORE THAN THAT, YOU CAN USE THE ENTIRE 8-INCH CAKE LAYER AND DOUBLE THE ICE CREAM AND MERINGUE AMOUNTS. LEFTOVER ALASKA CAN BE FROZEN FOR LATER NIBBLING.

• • •

FLAMING CHOCOLATE PRALINE ALASKA

1 Devil's Food Cake (recipe follows), trimmed to a 5-inch circle (reserve cake trimmings for later snacks)

1 pint of your favorite praline ice cream

4 egg whites

½ teaspoon cream of tartar

¾ cup sugar

High-quality chocolate sauce, optional

1 tablespoon 151 rum

Place the trimmed cake on a large freezer-to-oven plate, a pie pan turned upside down, or other metal, ovenproof tray or plate.

Soften the ice cream slightly and cut away the container. Turn it out onto a large piece of plastic wrap. Drape the ice cream with another large piece of plastic wrap and mold it into a dome shape, 5 inches in diameter at the base. Place the ice cream on the trimmed cake and immediately place it in the freezer while making the meringue. (The recipe can be prepared to this point up to 1 week in advance. Thoroughly wrap the cake and ice cream with plastic wrap and keep frozen.)

To make the meringue: In a grease-free mixer bowl, beat the egg whites on high speed until frothy. Add the cream of tartar and beat until the whites are just barely peaky. Beat in the sugar, 1 tablespoon at a time. Continue beating until stiff and glossy.

Remove the ice cream and cake base from the freezer and remove the plastic. With clean hands, pile the meringue on the frozen Alaska, covering all surfaces and swirling and making cute peaks in the meringue with your fingertips. Immediately place the Alaska back in the freezer, uncovered, and keep it frozen until ready to serve. (This step can be done up to 1 day in advance.)

Note: Be sure the Alaska is frozen for a minimum of 4 hours before proceeding to the next step.

Preheat the oven to 475°F. If desired, drizzle individual dessert plates with chocolate sauce. Place the Alaska in the oven for 4 to 6 minutes, or until the meringue is nicely browned all over and the tips are golden brown.

Bring to the table immediately and place on a trivet. Flame it immediately: Place the 151 rum in a metal ladle or large spoon and warm it over a candle. Then light the rum and carefully pour it over the Alaska. Be careful not to dribble any of the rum on the table or yourself—it is on fire!

When the flames go out, cut the Alaska into wedges and serve it on dessert plates.

For a Flaming Chocolate Cherry Alaska: Substitute chocolate cherry ice cream (I like Ben & Jerry's Cherry Garcia™) for the praline ice cream.

CHEF'S TIPS:
- *When making the meringue, don't start adding the sugar too soon, and don't add it too fast.*
- *Keep the whole Alaska really well frozen before baking the meringue in the oven.*

• • •

DEVIL'S FOOD CAKE

¾ **cup flour**

½ **cup sugar**

¼ **cup Dutch-process
cocoa powder**

½ **teaspoon baking powder**

**4 tablespoons
(½ stick) butter, softened**

1 teaspoon vanilla extract

1 egg

6 tablespoons sour cream

2 tablespoons milk

Preheat the oven to 350°F. Butter and flour an 8-inch round or square cake pan. Set aside.

In the bowl of a standing electric mixer or other large mixing bowl, sift together the flour, sugar, cocoa powder, and baking powder.

Add the remaining ingredients and mix on low speed until combined. Turn the mixer up to medium speed and mix until the batter is smooth, about 2 minutes. Scrape down the sides of the bowl as necessary.

Scrape the batter into the prepared pan and bake on the middle rack of the oven for 25 to 30 minutes, or until a cake tester or toothpick poked in the cake comes out clean.

Let the cake cool in the pan on a rack for 5 minutes, then run a knife around the side of the pan and turn the cake out onto a rack to cool thoroughly.

IF OLD-FASHIONED BREAD PUDDING ROCKS YOUR BOAT, YOU'LL LOVE THIS VARIATION MADE WITH EGGNOG INSTEAD OF CREAM. AND IT'S JUST AS GOOD BAKED A DAY AHEAD AND THEN REHEATED. SERVE IT DRIZZLED WITH RUM CARAMEL. FESTIVE, EASY, AND DELICIOUS!

. . .

EGGNOG BREAD PUDDING WITH RUM CARAMEL

8 cups packed ½-inch to 1-inch cubed rustic baguette or French bread

4 tablespoons (½ stick) butter, melted

¼ cup currants

¼ cup dried cranberries

1 cup sugar

2 egg yolks

4 large eggs

2¾ cups high-quality eggnog (not fat-free)

¾ teaspoon ground nutmeg

¼ cup dark rum

RUM CARAMEL

1 cup high-quality caramel sauce

2 tablespoons dark rum

.

Whipped cream for garnish

Place the bread cubes in a large bowl and drizzle with melted butter. Toss in the currants and dried cranberries.

In another bowl, whisk together the sugar, egg yolks, whole eggs, eggnog, nutmeg, and rum until well combined. Pour the egg mixture over the bread cubes and stir gently. Let the mixture sit for at least 30 minutes, poking the bread down into the egg mixture often and stirring it up every 10 minutes or so.

Preheat the oven to 350°F.

Place the bread pudding mixture in a 7- by 11-inch or 9-inch square glass baking pan. Bake for 40 minutes, or until the center is just barely set and a knife comes out clean.

To make the Rum Caramel: In a small bowl, whisk together the caramel sauce and rum. Serve the pudding warm, drizzled with some of the Rum Caramel. Garnish with a pouf of whipped cream. Serve additional Rum Caramel on the side.

CHEF'S TIPS:
If you won't be serving it immediately, the pudding can be cooled, covered, and refrigerated for up to 2 days. Remove 2 hours before reheating. Preheat the oven to 300°F. Heat the bread pudding, uncovered, for 10 to 15 minutes, or until just warm.

THESE WONDERFUL INDIVIDUAL TARTS ARE EASY TO MAKE, EVEN FOR THOSE WHO ARE "CRUST-INTIMIDATED." THE FINISHED TARTS ARE FREE-FORM, MEANING THEY ARE MADE WITHOUT ANY PANS, SO THE FINAL PRODUCT HAS A MORE RUSTIC LOOK THAN FORMAL PIES OR TARTS. THEY ARE BEST SERVED WHEN WARM, TOPPED WITH A SMALL SCOOP OF VANILLA ICE CREAM.

• • •

FREE-FORM PEAR & ALMOND TARTS

ALMOND CRUST

3 cups flour

½ cup sliced almonds, finely chopped

2 teaspoons sugar

1 teaspoon salt

8 tablespoons (1 stick) butter, cold, cut into small chunks

½ cup shortening, cold

1 large egg, beaten

4 teaspoons cider vinegar

6 tablespoons ice water

To make the Almond Crust: Mix the flour, almonds, sugar, and salt together in a large bowl. Add the butter and shortening and, with a pastry blender or clean hands, combine until the mixture forms pea-sized particles.

In a small, separate bowl, mix together 2 TABLESPOONS of the beaten egg, the vinegar, and the ice water. (Reserve the remaining beaten egg for egg wash.) Stir this mixture into the dry mixture and mix until the liquid is just incorporated. (This dough should be fairly moist and pliable, not crumbly. If the dough is too dry, add more ice water, 1 to 2 teaspoons at a time.)

Form the dough into a log and wrap in plastic wrap. Chill it in the refrigerator for 1 hour before rolling it out.

To make the Pear Filling: Place the pears in a large bowl. In a separate bowl, mix the sugar, flour, and cinnamon together and reserve.

Preheat the oven to 400°F. Lightly spray 2 or 3 large baking sheets with nonstick vegetable spray and set aside.

PEAR FILLING

2½ pounds ripe but firm Bartlett or Anjou pears, unpeeled, cored, and sliced lengthwise into ¼- to ½-inch slices (about 7½ cups)

¾ cup sugar

1½ tablespoons flour

½ teaspoon ground cinnamon

●

¼ cup (4 ounces) marzipan or almond paste, optional

Sugar for sprinkling on top, optional

After the dough has chilled, cut it into 8 equal portions. On a lightly floured surface, roll out 1 piece of dough into a ⅛-inch-thick circle. Keep the other pieces covered with waxed paper or plastic wrap while you work. Repeat with the remaining pieces of dough, keeping the rolled-out circles separate and covered.

Sprinkle the pears with the reserved sugar mixture and toss very gently. Coat the pears thoroughly; no dry mixture should be left in the bowl.

If using the marzipan or almond paste, divide it into ½-tablespoon pieces. Flatten out each piece and tear it into several pieces. Place the pieces on the tart shells.

Divide the Pear Filling among the tart shells, placing about ¾ heaping cup in the center of each. Gather up the crust edges around the filling, bringing about 1½ inches of pastry all around over the fruit to make an open-faced, rustic-looking tart.

With a spatula, carefully transfer each tart to a baking sheet. (You will be able to fit 3 or 4 tarts on each sheet.)

Whisk 1 teaspoon of water into the reserved beaten egg and lightly brush the exposed dough with the egg wash. Sprinkle the tarts lightly with sugar, if desired.

Bake for 30 to 32 minutes, or until the crust is cooked through and golden brown and the filling is bubbling.

CHEF'S TIPS:
● *It is very important to allow 1 hour for the Almond Crust to chill before rolling it out.*
● *The pears and dry ingredients are mixed at the last minute to avoid drawing too much liquid from the pears, which could make the crust soggy.*

FINALLY, A WAY TO USE THE LAVENDER FROM THAT BIG PLANT IN YOUR YARD! THIS SYRUP IS SO EASY TO MAKE, AND IT'S JUST THE THING TO GIVE YOUR FRESH FRUIT A SPECIAL TOUCH. MAKE EXTRA LAVENDER-INFUSED HONEY SYRUP TO GIVE AS PRETTY HOSTESS GIFTS. SEAL IN SMALL BOTTLES AND TIE A FRESH LAVENDER FLOWER TO EACH ONE.

• • •

SUCCULENT SUMMER STONE FRUITS WITH LAVENDER-INFUSED HONEY SYRUP

LAVENDER-INFUSED HONEY SYRUP

½ cup high-quality honey, preferably local

½ cup water

8 fresh lavender flowers, unsprayed, and rinsed (or use 1 tablespoon dried)

•

About 4 cups assorted fresh, ripe stone fruits, prepared as follows before measuring:

Peaches, peeled, pitted, and cut into wedges

Large apricots, pitted and cut into wedges

Plums, pitted and cut into wedges

Nectarines, pitted and cut into wedges

Dark or light sweet cherries, pitted

2 teaspoons fresh lemon juice

Fresh lavender flowers for garnish, optional

To make the Lavender-Infused Honey Syrup: In a small, heavy saucepan, combine the honey, water, and lavender flowers. Bring to a low boil over medium heat, being careful that the mixture does not foam up. Simmer slowly for about 10 minutes, or until the mixture is like thin pancake syrup. Remove from the heat and cool to room temperature. Strain into a glass jar, cover, and reserve. The syrup will keep, covered, at room temperature for 2 weeks.

To assemble and serve: In a large bowl, toss the fruit first with the lemon juice, then with the Lavender-Infused Honey Syrup. Serve in pretty glasses or fruit dishes, garnished with fresh lavender flowers, if desired.

Makes 8 servings

INSPIRED BY THE PREMIUM COFFEE CRAZE AND NAMED FOR MY HOME-TOWN OF SEATTLE, THIS DESSERT PLAYS ON BOTH THE TRADITIONAL ITALIAN CUSTARD RECIPE OF PANNA COTTA AND THE PACIFIC NORTHWEST'S MOCHA MADNESS!

• • •

"LATTE LAND" MOCHA PANNA COTTAS WITH MOCHA SUGAR COOKIES

PANNA COTTAS

1 tablespoon powdered gelatin

¼ cup water

2 tablespoons instant espresso powder or instant coffee powder

1 cup cream

¾ cup sugar

¾ cup sour cream

1½ cups mascarpone

1½ teaspoons vanilla extract

½ cup high-quality chocolate sauce

ESPRESSO CHOCOLATE SAUCE

¼ cup high-quality chocolate sauce

1 tablespoon brewed espresso or strong coffee

•

Lightly sweetened whipped cream for garnish

Mocha Sugar Cookies (recipe follows)

To make the Panna Cottas: In a small, microwave-safe bowl, sprinkle the gelatin over 2 tablespoons of the water. Soak until the gelatin is soft, then microwave on high power for only about 2 seconds, or until the gelatin is melted but not foaming up.

In a small bowl, combine the espresso powder with the remaining 2 tablespoons water. In a large mixing bowl, combine the cream, sugar, sour cream, mascarpone, vanilla, and chocolate sauce. Add the espresso mixture and the gelatin and mix well.

Place the mixing bowl over a pan of simmering water. Cook the mixture, whisking constantly, until smooth and hot (150° to 160°F on an instant-read thermometer).

Remove from the heat and divide the mixture evenly among 8 coffee cups. Cover the cups with plastic wrap, making sure the plastic does not touch the custard. Refrigerate for a minimum of 12 hours to set.

To make the Espresso Chocolate Sauce: Mix the chocolate sauce and brewed coffee well. Hold the sauce at room temperature. It can be made the day before.

To serve: Top each cup of Panna Cotta with some of the Espresso Chocolate Sauce, then dollop it with lightly sweetened whipped cream. Serve each "coffee cup" on a saucer or larger plate, with a couple of Mocha Sugar Cookies alongside.

MOCHA SUGAR COOKIES

⅓ cup shortening

½ cup packed
brown sugar

½ cup granulated sugar

1 egg

1½ teaspoons
vanilla extract

1 tablespoon milk

2 tablespoons instant
espresso powder or instant
coffee powder

2 cups flour

½ teaspoon salt

\½ teaspoon baking soda

¼ teaspoon
baking powder

1 (1.75- to 2-ounce)
semisweet chocolate bar,
coarsely grated

Preheat the oven to 375°F.

In a mixer, cream together the shortening and brown and granulated sugars. Add the egg and vanilla and mix briefly. Warm the milk and stir in the espresso powder. Add this to the creamed mixture, and mix until well incorporated.

Sift the flour, salt, baking soda, and baking powder together and add to the creamed mixture. Mix until well incorporated.

Roll the dough into 1-inch balls and place them 2 inches apart on an ungreased baking sheet. Flatten each cookie with the bottom of a lightly buttered glass dipped in sugar, or press with a fork. Sprinkle lightly with the grated chocolate and bake for 8 to 10 minutes. Remove from the oven, allow the cookies to cool for about 3 minutes on the baking sheet, then carefully transfer the cookies to a rack to cool completely.

CHEF'S TIPS:
If you're having lots of guests for dinner, prepare this recipe in tiny espresso or demitasse cups—for a delicious "little something."

Makes about 2 dozen

THESE ARE FUN GARNISHES FOR DESSERTS OR EVEN TO EAT PLAIN. THIS RECIPE MAKES LOTS OF STRAWS, SO DON'T WORRY IF YOU BREAK A COUPLE WHEN REMOVING THEM FROM THE PAN—THE MORE RUSTIC AND IRREGULAR THE PIECES, THE MORE FUN.

• • •

COCOA MERINGUE STRAWS

2 large or 3 small egg whites, free of any egg yolk

⅛ teaspoon cream of tartar

¼ cup granulated sugar

¼ cup powdered sugar

1 tablespoon unsweetened cocoa powder

Preheat the oven to 275°F.

Place the egg whites in a grease-free (not plastic) mixer bowl.

In a mixer with a whip attachment, whip the egg whites on medium-high speed for about 2 minutes. Mix the cream of tartar and granulated sugar together, then gradually add the granulated sugar mixture to the egg whites while continuing to beat. When all the granulated sugar is incorporated (it should take about 1 minute), slowly add the powdered sugar and then the cocoa powder while continuing to whip. Whip the meringue until stiff peaks form. Total whipping time should be about 4½ minutes.

Place the meringue in a pastry bag fitted with a #3 plain tip. Line a baking sheet with parchment and place it on the counter with a long side toward you. Pipe the meringue into 10-inch straws on the baking sheet. You should be able to pipe 8 to 10 straws onto the sheet.

Bake the meringues for 1 hour, then turn off the heat and leave them in the oven until they are very dry, an additional hour or up to overnight.

Very carefully remove the meringues from the parchment paper, pulling back the paper or using a metal spatula. Your goal is to break each straw into only 3 pieces, but use whatever size pieces you end up with!

Store the totally cooled meringues in an airtight container cushioned with paper towels. Or leave the meringues on the baking pan and wrap the whole thing tightly with plastic wrap.

CHEF'S TIPS:
To remove traces of grease from the bowl you use for whipping egg whites, rinse the bowl in very, very hot water, then allow it to cool thoroughly and/or wipe the bowl out with a clean cloth moistened in distilled vinegar.

INDEX

A–B

Aioli
    Hazelnut Aioli, for Grilled Asparagus, 129
Almonds
    Free-Form Pear & Almond Tarts, 194–95
    Hot Buttery Almond Rum, 47

Thai Curry–Spiced Stuffed Eggs with
    Shrimp, 52
Tropical Ceviche, 75
Warm Almond-Crusted Brie with Apple-
    Onion Compote, 54–55
Apples
    Apple-Onion Compote, for Warm Almond-
    Crusted Brie, 54–55
    Gala Apple, Blue Cheese & Toasted Pecan
    Salad with Cider Vinaigrette, 87

Appetizers, 49–75
    Blue Cheese & Hazelnut-Stuffed
      Mushrooms, 74
    Chili-Roasted Cashews, 57
    Chipotle Deviled Eggs, 51
    Crab Towers, 63–65
    Grilled Bread with Bruschetta Tomatoes, 53
    Herbed Crostini, 71
    Parmesan Poppy Seed Cheese Puffs, 60–61
    Prosciutto-Wrapped Melon with White
      Balsamic & Honey Mint Drizzle, 56
    Sesame Cheddar Olive Poppers, 66
    Sexy Baked Olives & Feta Cheese, 72
    Smoked Salmon with Wasabi Cream Cheese
      & Ginger Pickled Onions on Homemade
      Crackers, 68–70
    Steamed Mussels in Thai Basil Coconut
      Broth, 58

Unbelievable Apple Cake with Cider Crème
    Anglaise & Cranberry Compote, 176–77
Apricots
    Succulent Summer Stone Fruits with
    Lavender-Infused Honey Syrup, 197
Arugula
    Shaved Fennel & Arugula Salad with Lemon
    Vinaigrette, 81
Asparagus
    Grilled Asparagus with Hazelnut Aioli, 129
Banana Walnut Cake, for Tropical Fruit
    Shortcake, 173
Barbecue sauce
    Red Eye Barbecue Sauce, for Classic Meat
    Loaf, 153
Beef
    Classic Meat Loaf with Red Eye Barbecue
    Sauce, 152–53

Roasted Beef Tenderloin for a Crowd with
Horseradish Mustard Crust, 106
Seared Steak with Chipotle Mushrooms &
Crema, 102 3
Sunday Slow-Cooked Roast Beef with Half a
Bottle of Wine & 20 Cloves of Garlic, 157
Berries
Billowing Strawberry Poppy Seed Layer Cake,
185–86
Blackberry-Honey Vinaigrette, for Baby
Greens, 96

Bok choy
Toasted Garlic & Ginger Soy-Glazed Bok
Choy, 134
Bourbon Whipped Cream, for "Gimme Both"
Pumpkin-Pecan Pie, 189
Bread
Grilled Bread with Bruschetta Tomatoes, 53
Herbed Crostini, 71
Bread pudding
Eggnog Bread Pudding with Rum
Caramel, 193

"Chef-Style" Berry or Fruit Purée, 187
Fresh Berries with Fluffy Vin Santo Zabaglione
& Hazelnut Biscotti, 178–79
Juicy Strawberry Pineapple Sangría, 40
Pan-Sized Berry Pancakes with Citrus Syrup,
161–62
See also Cranberries
Beverages. See Drinks
Biscotti
Hazelnut Biscotti, for Fresh Berries with Fluffy
Vin Santo Zabaglione, 179
Blue cheese
Blue Cheese & Beer Dressing, for Wedge
O'Lettuce, 94
Blue Cheese & Hazelnut–Stuffed
Mushrooms, 74
Blue Cheese Scalloped Potatoes, 145
Gala Apple, Blue Cheese & Toasted Pecan
Salad with Cider Vinaigrette, 87

Brie
Warm Almond-Crusted Brie with Apple-
Onion Compote, 54–55
Bruschetta
Grilled Bread with Bruschetta Tomatoes, 53
Brussels Sprouts with Toasted Walnut Butter, 141
Butter
Parsley Butter, for Chicken & Mushroom
Stroganoff, 166
Spicy Orange-Ginger Butter, for Roasted King
Salmon, 114
Thai Lime Butter, for Roasted Shrimp, 101
Toasted Walnut Butter, for Brussels
Sprouts, 141
Butter Lettuce & Endive Salad with Avocado,
Grapefruit & Pomegranate Seeds, 91

C–D

Cabbage, red
  Sweet & Sour Ruby Cabbage, 139
Cake
  Banana Walnut Cake, for Tropical Fruit
    Shortcake, 173
  Billowing Strawberry Poppy Seed Layer Cake,
    185–86
  Devil's Food Cake, for Flaming Chocolate
    Praline Alaska, 192
  Oozy Chocolate Grand Marnier Cakes with
    Glazed Blood Oranges, 180–82
  Unbelievable Apple Cake with Cider Crème
    Anglaise & Cranberry Compote, 176–77
Caramel sauce
  Rum Caramel, for Eggnog Bread Pudding, 193
Cashews
  Chili-Roasted Cashews, 57
Ceviche
  Tropical Ceviche, 75
Champagne Vinaigrette, for Butter Lettuce &
  Endive Salad, 91
Chard
  Balsamic Braised Greens, 144
Cheese
  Blue Cheese & Beer Dressing, for Wedge
    O'Lettuce, 94
  Blue Cheese & Hazelnut–Stuffed
    Mushrooms, 74
  Blue Cheese Scalloped Potatoes, 145
  Gala Apple, Blue Cheese & Toasted Pecan
    Salad with Cider Vinaigrette, 87
  Parmesan Poppy Seed Cheese Puffs, 60–61
  Sesame Cheddar Olive Poppers, 66
  Sexy Baked Olives & Feta Cheese, 72
  Tam's White Heat Mac & Cheese, 164–65
  Warm Almond-Crusted Brie with Apple-
    Onion Compote, 54–55
Cherries
  Cherries Jubilee Parfaits, 183
  Cherry Compote, for Cherries Jubilee
    Parfaits, 183
  Drunken Cherries, for Dubious Manhattan, 37
  Flaming Chocolate Cherry Alaska
    (variation), 191

Chicken
  Chardonnay Braised Chicken, 110–11
  Chicken, Artichoke & Parmesan Baked
    Penne, 154
  Chicken & Mushroom Stroganoff with Parsley
    Noodles, 166–68
  Herb-Marinated Grilled Chicken Breasts, 105
  Pacific Rim Chicken Pot, 163
Chili-Roasted Cashews, 57
Chipotle
  Chipotle Deviled Eggs, 51
  purée, 25
  Seared Steak with Chipotle Mushrooms &
    Crema, 102–3
  Spicy Chipotle "French" Dressing, for Wedge
    O'Lettuce, 95
Chocolate
  Cocoa Meringue Straws, 200–1
  Devil's Food Cake, for Flaming Chocolate
    Praline Alaska, 192
  Espresso Chocolate Sauce, for "Latte Land"
    Mocha Panna Cottas, 198
  Flaming Chocolate Praline Alaska, 190–92
  Oozy Chocolate Grand Marnier Cakes with
    Glazed Blood Oranges, 180–82
Cider
  Cider Crème Anglaise, for Unbelievable
    Apple Cake, 177
  Cider Vinaigrette, for Gala Apple, Blue
    Cheese & Toasted Pecan Salad, 87
Citrus Syrup, for Pan-Sized Berry Pancakes, 162
Clams
  "Stinking Rose" Clam Pasta, 119
Cocoa Meringue Straws, 200–1
Coconut
  Coconut Cream, for Tropical Fruit
    Shortcake, 173
  Coconutty Adult Mocha, 46
Coffee
  Coconutty Adult Mocha, 46
  Espresso Chocolate Sauce, for "Latte Land"
    Mocha Panna Cottas, 198
  "Latte Land" Mocha Panna Cottas with
    Mocha Sugar Cookies, 198–99
  Mocha Sugar Cookies, for "Latte Land"
    Mocha Panna Cottas, 199

Compote
    Apple-Onion Compote, for Warm Almond-
        Crusted Brie, 54–55
    Cherry Compote, for Cherries Jubilee
        Parfaits, 183
    Cranberry Compote, for Unbelievable Apple
        Cake, 177
Cookies
    Cocoa Meringue Straws, 200–1
    Hazelnut Biscotti, for Fresh Berries with Fluffy
        Vin Santo Zabaglione, 179
    Mocha Sugar Cookies, for "Latte Land"
        Mocha Panna Cottas, 199
Corn
    Creamy Double-Corn Polenta, 142
    Sweet Pepper & Corn Relish, for Crab Soufflé
        Cakes, 109
    Tomato-Corn Summer Salsa, for Cumin-
        Grilled Zucchini, 143
Crab
    Crab Soufflé Cakes with Sweet Pepper &
        Corn Relish, 108–9
    Crab Towers, 63–65
Crackers
    Homemade Crackers, for Smoked Salmon, 69
Cranberries
    Cranberry Compote, for Unbelievable Apple
        Cake, 177
    Cranberry Pickled Pumpkin, 131
    Cranberry Vinaigrette, for Seasonal Greens, 90
Cream
    Bourbon Whipped Cream, for "Gimme Both"
        Pumpkin-Pecan Pie, 189
    Coconut Cream, for Tropical Fruit
        Shortcake, 173
    Lemon Cream, for Frozen "Lemon Drop"
        Ice, 174
    Maple Cream, for Maple Scalloped Sweet
        Potatoes with Sage, 130
    Orange Cream, for Oozy Chocolate Grand
        Marnier Cakes, 183
Cream cheese
    Wasabi Cream Cheese, for Smoked Salmon, 68
Crostini
    Herbed Crostini, 71

Crust
    Almond Crust, for Free-Form Pear & Almond
        Tarts, 194
    Classic Flaky Pie Crust, for "Gimme Both"
        Pumpkin-Pecan Pie, 189
Custard
    Cider Crème Anglaise, for Unbelievable
        Apple Cakes, 177
    Fluffy Vin Santo Zabaglione, for Fresh
        Berries, 178
Dessert, 171–201
    Billowing Strawberry Poppy Seed Layer Cake,
        185–86
    Cherries Jubilee Parfaits, 183
    Cocoa Meringue Straws, 200–1
    Eggnog Bread Pudding with Rum Caramel, 193
    Flaming Chocolate Cherry Alaska
        (variation), 191
    Flaming Chocolate Praline Alaska, 190–92
    Free-Form Pear & Almond Tarts, 194–95
    Fresh Berries with Fluffy Vin Santo Zabaglione
        & Hazelnut Biscotti, 178–79
    Frozen "Lemon Drop" Ice Topped with a
        Lemon Cream Cloud, 174
    "Gimme Both" Pumpkin-Pecan Pie with
        Bourbon Whipped Cream, 188–89
    "Latte Land" Mocha Panna Cottas with
        Mocha Sugar Cookies, 198–99
    Oozy Chocolate Grand Marnier Cakes with
        Glazed Blood Oranges, 180–82
    Succulent Summer Stone Fruits with
        Lavender-Infused Honey Syrup, 197
    Tropical Fruit Shortcake with Coconut Cream,
        172–73
    Unbelievable Apple Cake with Cider Crème
        Anglaise & Cranberry Compote, 176–77
Dressing. See Salad dressing
Drinks, 27–47
    Autumn Sidecar, 37
    Coconutty Adult Mocha, 46
    Cosmo Chi Chi, 31
    Dubious Manhattan with Drunken Cherries, 37
    Ginger Jasmine Lime Rickey, 41
    Homemade Sweet & Sour, 28
    Hot Buttery Almond Rum, 47
    Juicy Strawberry Pineapple Sangría, 40
    Mahali's Sky, 42
    Melon Mélange, 34

Perfect Ten 75, 29
Rosemary Rhubarb Meyer Lemonade, 32–33
Rosy 'Rita, 29
Sake Punch, 45
Terrific Classic 'Tini, 36
Tropical Sweet & Sour, 31
Winter Spiced White Wine, 35

E–F

Eggnog Bread Pudding with Rum Caramel, 193
Eggplant
    Roasted Vegetable Risotto, 118
Eggs
    Chipotle Deviled Eggs, 51
    Thai Curry–Spiced Stuffed Eggs with
        Shrimp, 52
Endive
    Butter Lettuce & Endive Salad with Avocado,
        Grapefruit & Pomegranate Seeds, 91
Escarole
    Balsamic Braised Greens, 144
Espresso Chocolate Sauce, for "Latte Land"
    Mocha Panna Cottas, 198
Fennel
    Roasted Pork Loin with Fennel Spice Rub, 115
    Shaved Fennel & Arugula Salad with Lemon
        Vinaigrette, 81
Fish
    Grilled Halibut with Lemon-Herb Splash, 104
    Roasted King Salmon with Orange-Ginger
        Salsa, 113–14
    Tropical Ceviche, 75
Fruit
    "Chef-Style" Berry or Fruit Purée, 187
    Pan-Sized Berry Pancakes with Citrus Syrup,
        161–62
    Succulent Summer Stone Fruits with
        Lavender-Infused Honey Syrup, 197
    Tropical Fruit Shortcake with Coconut Cream,
        172–73
    See also individual fruits

G–H

Garlic
    Confetti Garlic Mashed Potatoes, 146
    Sunday Slow-Cooked Roast Beef with Half a
        Bottle of Wine & 20 Cloves of Garlic, 157

Gazpacho
    Best of the Season Gazpacho, 97
    Gazpacho Salsa, for Crab Towers, 63–64
General recipe notes, 25
Ginger
    Ginger Jasmine Lime Rickey, 41
    Ginger Pickled Onions, for Smoked Salmon, 70
    Orange-Ginger Salsa, for Roasted King
        Salmon, 114
    Spicy Orange-Ginger Butter, for Roasted King
        Salmon, 114
Glaze
    Red Wine Glaze, for Seared Lamb, 123
Gravy
    Old-Fashioned Turkey Mushroom Gravy, for
        Roast Turkey, 159
Green Goddess Dressing, for Wedge O'Lettuce, 92
Grilled dishes
    Charlotte's Greek Grilled Pita Salad, 83
    Cumin-Grilled Zucchini with Tomato-Corn
        Summer Salsa, 143
    Grilled Asparagus with Hazelnut Aioli, 129
    Grilled Bread with Bruschetta Tomatoes, 53
    Grilled Halibut with Lemon-Herb Splash, 104
    Herb-Marinated Grilled Chicken Breasts, 105
Halibut
    Grilled Halibut with Lemon-Herb Splash, 104
Hazelnuts
    Hazelnut Aioli, for Grilled Asparagus, 129
    Hazelnut Biscotti, for Fresh Berries with Fluffy
        Vin Santo Zabaglione, 179
    toasting, 25
Herbs
    Herb Butter, for New Century Lobster
        Américaine, 124–5
    Herbed Crostini, 71
    Herb-Marinated Grilled Chicken Breasts, 105
    Lavender-Infused Honey Syrup, for Succulent
        Summer Stone Fruits, 197
    Lemon-Herb Splash, for Grilled Halibut, 104
    Minted Herb Salad, for Seared Lamb, 123
    Parsley Butter, for Chicken & Mushroom
        Stroganoff, 166
    Rosemary Rhubarb Meyer Lemonade, 32–33
Honey
    Blackberry-Honey Vinaigrette, for Baby
        Greens, 96

Lavender-Infused Honey Syrup, for Succulent
  Summer Stone Fruits, 197
Sesame Honey Dressing, for Warm Spinach
  Salad, 85
White Balsamic & Honey Mint Drizzle, for
  Prosciutto-Wrapped Melon, 56
Horseradish Mustard Crust, for Beef
  Tenderloin, 106

I–L

Ice
  Frozen "Lemon Drop" Ice Topped with a
    Lemon Cream Cloud, 174
Kale
  Balsamic Braised Greens, 144
Lamb
  Seared Lamb with Olive Jus & Minted Herb
    Salad, 121–23
Lavender-Infused Honey Syrup, for Succulent
  Summer Stone Fruits, 197
Lemon
  Citrus Syrup, for Pan-Sized Berry Pancakes, 162
  Fresh Lemon Sour (variation), 28
  Frozen "Lemon Drop" Ice Topped with a
    Lemon Cream Cloud, 174
  Lemon-Herb Splash, for Grilled Halibut, 104
  Lemon-Spiked Basmati Rice, 133
  Lemon Vinaigrette, for Shaved Fennel &
    Arugula Salad, 81
  Rosemary Rhubarb Meyer Lemonade, 32–33
  zest, 25
Lime
  Fresh Lime Sour (variation), 28
  Ginger Jasmine Lime Rickey, 41
  Lime-Spiked Basmati Rice (variation), 133
  Lime Syrup, for Ginger Jasmine Lime Rickey, 41
  Thai Lime Butter, for Roasted Shrimp, 101
Lobster
  New Century Lobster Américaine Poached in
    Herb Butter, 124–25

M–N

Macaroni
  Tam's White Heat Mac & Cheese, 164–65
Main course, 99–125
  Chardonnay Braised Chicken, 110–11

  Chicken, Artichoke & Parmesan Baked
    Penne, 154
  Chicken & Mushroom Stroganoff with Parsley
    Noodles, 166–68
  Classic Meat Loaf with Red Eye Barbecue
    Sauce, 152–53
  Crab Soufflé Cakes with Sweet Pepper &
    Corn Relish, 108–9
  Grilled Halibut with Lemon-Herb Splash, 104
  Herb-Marinated Grilled Chicken Breasts, 105
  New Century Lobster Américaine Poached in
    Herb Butter, 124–25
  Pacific Rim Chicken Pot, 163
  Roasted Beef Tenderloin for a Crowd with
    Horseradish Mustard Crust, 106
  Roasted King Salmon with Orange-Ginger
    Salsa, 113–14
  Roasted Pork Loin with Fennel Spice Rub, 115
  Roasted Shrimp with Thai Lime Butter, 101
  Roasted Vegetable Risotto, 116–18
  Roast Turkey with Old-Fashioned Turkey
    Mushroom Gravy, 158–59
  Seared Lamb with Olive Jus & Minted Herb
    Salad, 121–23
  Seared Steak with Chipotle Mushrooms &
    Crema, 102–3
  Slow-Braised Pork Pot Roast with Apples &
    Onions, 169
  "Stinking Rose" Clam Pasta, 119
  Sunday Slow-Cooked Roast Beef with Half a
    Bottle of Wine & 20 Cloves of Garlic, 157
  Tam's White Heat Mac & Cheese, 164–65
Manhattan
  Dubious Manhattan with Drunken Cherries, 37
Maple Cream, for Maple Scalloped Sweet
  Potatoes with Sage, 130
Margarita
  Rosy 'Rita, 29
Marinade
  Herb Marinade, for Grilled Chicken
    Breasts, 105
Martini
  Terrific Classic 'Tini, 36
Meat loaf
  Classic Meat Loaf with Red Eye Barbecue
    Sauce, 152–53
Melon
  Melon Mélange, 34

Prosciutto-Wrapped Melon with White
    Balsamic & Honey Mint Drizzle, 56
Menus, 1–25
    Autumn Fireside Dinner, 24
    Big Holiday Feast, The, 19
    Dinner Party with Friends, 8
    Fabulous Fall Dinner for Six, 10
    Fiesta with Friends, 16
    First Taste of Summer Celebration, 9
    Inexpensive Fancy Pants "Faux French"
        Dinner, 17
    New Classics Cocktail Party, 13
    Pacific Rim Party, 9
    Posh Patio "Picnic," 11
    Remembering Sunday Dinner, 11
    Romantic Dinner, 7
    "Share the Work" Summer Entertaining, 22
    Simple Summer Supper, 23
    Surprise Breakfast in Bed, 17
    Tiki Torch Dreamin', 24
Meringue
    Cocoa Meringue Straws, 200–1
Mint
    Mint Oil, for Seared Lamb, 123
    Minted Herb Salad, for Seared Lamb, 123
    White Balsamic & Honey Mint Drizzle, for
        Prosciutto-Wrapped Melon, 56
Mocha
    Coconutty Adult Mocha, 46
    "Latte Land" Mocha Panna Cottas with
        Mocha Sugar Cookies, 198–99
Mushrooms
    Blue Cheese & Hazelnut-Stuffed
        Mushrooms, 74
    Chipotle Mushrooms & Crema, for Seared
        Steak, 103
    Old-Fashioned Turkey Mushroom Gravy, for
        Roast Turkey, 159
    Warm Spinach Salad with Shiitake
        Mushrooms, Sweet Peppers & Sesame
        Honey Dressing, 84–85
    Wild Mushroom Risotto, 136–37
Mussels
    Steamed Mussels in Thai Basil Coconut
        Broth, 58
Mustard
    Horseradish Mustard Crust, for Beef
        Tenderloin, 106

Nectarines
    "Chef-Style" Berry or Fruit Purée, 187
    Succulent Summer Stone Fruits with
        Lavender-Infused Honey Syrup, 197
Noodles. See Pasta
Nuts
    Chili-Roasted Cashews, 57
    Free-Form Pear & Almond Tarts, 194–95
    "Gimme Both" Pumpkin-Pecan Pie with
        Bourbon Whipped Cream, 188–89
    Hazelnut Aioli, for Grilled Asparagus, 129
    Hazelnut Biscotti, for Fresh Berries with Vin
        Santo Zabaglione, 179
    Spicy Walnuts, for Seasonal Greens, 88
    Toasted Walnut Butter, for Brussels
        Sprouts, 141
    toasting hazelnuts, 25

O–R

Oil
    Herb Oil, for Herbed Crostini, 71
    Mint Oil, for Seared Lamb, 123
Olives
    Olive Compound, for Seared Lamb, 122
    Sesame Cheddar Olive Poppers, 66
    Sexy Baked Olives & Feta Cheese, 72
Onions
    Apple-Onion Compote, for Warm Almond-
        Crusted Brie, 55
    Ginger Pickled Onions, for Smoked Salmon, 70
Orange
    Glazed Blood Oranges, for Oozy Chocolate
        Grand Marnier Cakes, 182
    Orange Cream, for Oozy Chocolate Grand
        Marnier Cakes, 183
    Orange-Ginger Salsa, for Roasted King
        Salmon, 114
    Spicy Orange-Ginger Butter, for Roasted King
        Salmon, 114
Pancakes
    Pan-Sized Berry Pancakes with Citrus Syrup,
        161–62
Panna cotta
    "Latte Land" Mocha Panna Cottas with
        Mocha Sugar Cookies, 198–99
Parfait
    Cherries Jubilee Parfaits, 183

Parmesan Poppy Seed Cheese Puffs, 60–61
Parsley Butter, for Chicken & Mushroom
  Stroganoff, 166
Pasta
  Chicken, Artichoke & Parmesan Baked
    Penne, 154
  Parsley Noodles, for Chicken & Mushroom
    Stroganoff, 166–68
  "Stinking Rose" Clam Pasta, 119
  Tam's White Heat Mac & Cheese, 164–65
Peaches
  "Chef-Style" Berry or Fruit Purée, 187
  Succulent Summer Stone Fruits with
    Lavender-Infused Honey Syrup, 197
Pears
  Free-Form Pear & Almond Tarts, 194–95
  Seasonal Greens with Spicy Walnuts, Crisp
    Asian Pears & Cranberry Vinaigrette, 88–90
Pecans
  "Gimme Both" Pumpkin-Pecan Pie with
    Bourbon Whipped Cream, 188–89
Peppers
  Roasted Vegetable Risotto, 118
  Sweet Pepper & Corn Relish, 109
  Warm Spinach Salad with Shiitake
    Mushrooms, Sweet Peppers & Sesame
    Honey Dressing, 84–85
  See also Chipotle
Pickles
  Cranberry Pickled Pumpkin, 131
  Ginger Pickled Onions, for Smoked Salmon, 70
Pie
  "Gimme Both" Pumpkin-Pecan Pie with
    Bourbon Whipped Cream, 188–89
  See also Tarts, Crust
Pineapple
  Juicy Strawberry Pineapple Sangría, 40
  Tropical Fruit Shortcake with Coconut Cream,
    172–73
Pita
  Charlotte's Greek Grilled Pita Salad, 83
  Pita Chips, for Sexy Baked Olives & Feta, 73
Plums
  Succulent Summer Stone Fruits with
    Lavender-Infused Honey Syrup, 197
Polenta
  Creamy Double-Corn Polenta, 142

Poppy seeds
  Billowing Strawberry Poppy Seed Layer Cake,
    185–86
Pork
  Roasted Pork Loin with Fennel Spice Rub, 115
  Slow-Braised Pork Pot Roast with Apples &
    Onions, 169
Pot roast
  Slow-Braised Pork Pot Roast with Apples &
    Onions, 169
  Sunday Slow-Cooked Roast Beef with Half a
    Bottle of Wine & 20 Cloves of Garlic, 157
Potatoes
  Blue Cheese Scalloped Potatoes, 145
  Confetti Garlic Mashed Potatoes, 146
  Wasabi Mashed Potatoes, 135
Prosciutto-Wrapped Melon with White Balsamic
  & Honey Mint Drizzle, 56
Pumpkin
  Cranberry Pickled Pumpkin, 131
  "Gimme Both" Pumpkin-Pecan Pie with
    Bourbon Whipped Cream, 188–89
Punch
  Sake Punch, 45
Purée
  "Chef-Style" Berry or Fruit Purée, 187
  chipotle pepper purée, 25
Relish
  Sweet Pepper & Corn Relish, for Crab Soufflé
    Cakes, 109
Rhubarb
  Rosemary Rhubarb Meyer Lemonade, 32–33
Rice
  Colorful Jasmine Rice, 140
  Lemon-Spiked Basmati Rice, 133
  Lime-Spiked Basmati Rice (variation), 133
  Roasted Vegetable Risotto, 116–18
  Wild Mushroom Risotto, 136–37
Risotto
  Roasted Vegetable Risotto, 116–18
  Wild Mushroom Risotto, 136–37
Rosemary Rhubarb Meyer Lemonade, 32–33
Rub
  Fennel Spice Rub, for Roasted Pork Loin, 115
Rum Caramel, for Eggnog Bread Pudding, 193

S–T

Sake Punch, 45
Salad
    Baby Greens with Blackberry-Honey
      Vinaigrette, Toasted Hazelnuts & Chèvre, 96
    Butter Lettuce & Endive Salad with Avocado,
      Grapefruit & Pomegranate Seeds, 91
    Charlotte's Greek Grilled Pita Salad, 83
    Gala Apple, Blue Cheese & Toasted Pecan
      Salad with Cider Vinaigrette, 87
    Herb Salad, for Seared Lamb, 123
    Seasonal Greens with Spicy Walnuts, Crisp
      Asian Pears & Cranberry Vinaigrette, 88–90
    Shaved Fennel & Arugula Salad with Lemon
      Vinaigrette, 81
    Warm Spinach Salad with Shiitake
      Mushrooms, Sweet Peppers & Sesame
      Honey Dressing, 84–85
    Wedge O'Lettuce with Retro Dressings, 92–95
Salad dressing
    Blue Cheese & Beer Dressing, for Wedge
      O'Lettuce, 94
    Green Goddess Dressing, for Wedge
      O'Lettuce, 92
    Sesame Honey Dressing, for Warm Spinach
      Salad, 85
    Spicy Chipotle "French" Dressing, for Wedge
      O'Lettuce, 95
    See also Vinaigrette
Salmon
    Roasted King Salmon with Orange-Ginger
      Salsa, 113–14
    Smoked Salmon with Wasabi Cream Cheese
      & Ginger Pickled Onions on Homemade
      Crackers, 68–70
Salsa
    Gazpacho Salsa, for Crab Towers, 63–64
    Orange-Ginger Salsa, for Roasted King
      Salmon, 114
    Tomato-Corn Summer Salsa, for Cumin-
      Grilled Zucchini, 143
Sangría
    Juicy Strawberry Pineapple Sangría, 40
Sauce
    Espresso Chocolate Sauce, for "Latte Land"
      Mocha Panna Cottas, 198
    Hazelnut Aioli, for Grilled Asparagus, 129
    Red Eye Barbecue Sauce, for Classic Meat
      Loaf, 153
    Rum Caramel, for Eggnog Bread Pudding, 193
Scallops
    Tropical Ceviche, 75
Sesame seeds
    Sesame Cheddar Olive Poppers, 66
    Sesame Honey Dressing, for Warm Spinach
      Salad, 85
Shrimp
    Roasted Shrimp with Thai Lime Butter, 101
    Shrimp Won Ton Soup with Lemongrass, 86
Side dishes, 127–49
    Balsamic Braised Greens, 144
    Blue Cheese Scalloped Potatoes, 145
    Brussels Sprouts with Toasted Walnut
      Butter, 141
    Colorful Jasmine Rice, 140
    Confetti Garlic Mashed Potatoes, 146
    Cranberry Pickled Pumpkin, 131
    Creamy Double-Corn Polenta, 142
    Grilled Asparagus with Hazelnut Aioli, 129
    Lemon-Spiked Basmati Rice, 133
    Lime-Spiked Basmati Rice (variation), 133
    Sweet & Sour Ruby Cabbage, 139
    Toasted Garlic & Ginger Soy-Glazed Bok
      Choy, 134
    Ultimate Mom's Turkey Stuffing for a Crowd,
      148–49
    Wasabi Mashed Potatoes, 135
    Wild Mushroom Risotto, 136–37
Sidecar
    Autumn Sidecar, 37
Simple Syrup, 28
Soup
    Best of the Season Gazpacho, 97
    Rich Turkey Stock, 149
    Shrimp Won Ton Soup with Lemongrass, 86
    Spiced Squash Bisque, 79–80
Spinach
    Warm Spinach Salad with Shiitake
      Mushrooms, Sweet Peppers & Sesame
      Honey Dressing, 84–85
Squash
    Spiced Squash Bisque, 79–80
Squash seeds
    Crispy Seeds, for Spiced Squash Bisque, 80

Stock
    Rich Turkey Stock, 149
Strawberries
    Billowing Strawberry Poppy Seed Layer Cake, 185–86
    Juicy Strawberry Pineapple Sangría, 40
Stuffing
    Ultimate Mom's Turkey Stuffing for a Crowd, 148–49
Sweet & Sour
    Homemade, 28
    Tropical, for Cosmo Chi Chi, 31
Sweet potatoes
    Maple Scalloped Sweet Potatoes with Sage, 130
Syrup
    Citrus Syrup, for Pan-Sized Berry Pancakes, 162
    Lavender-Infused Honey Syrup, for Succulent Summer Stone Fruits, 197
    Lime Syrup, for Ginger Jasmine Lime Rickey, 41
    Simple Syrup, for Homemade Sweet & Sour, 28
Tarts
    Free-Form Pear & Almond Tarts, 194–95
Tomatoes
    Grilled Bread with Bruschetta Tomatoes, 53
    Tomato-Corn Summer Salsa, for Cumin-Grilled Zucchini, 143
Turkey
    Rich Turkey Stock, 149
    Roast Turkey with Old-Fashioned Turkey Mushroom Gravy, 158–59
    Ultimate Mom's Turkey Stuffing for a Crowd, 148–49
Turnip greens
    Balsamic Braised Greens, 144

U–Z

Vegetables
    Balsamic Braised Greens, 144
    Blue Cheese Scalloped Potatoes, 145
    Brussels Sprouts with Toasted Walnut Butter, 141
    Confetti Garlic Mashed Potatoes, 146
    Cranberry Pickled Pumpkin, 131
    Creamy Double-Corn Polenta, 142
    Cumin-Grilled Zucchini with Tomato-Corn Summer Salsa, 143

Grilled Asparagus with Hazelnut Aioli, 129
Maple Scalloped Sweet Potatoes with Sage, 130
Roasted Vegetable Risotto, 116–18
Sweet & Sour Ruby Cabbage, 139
Toasted Garlic & Ginger Soy-Glazed Bok Choy, 134
Wasabi Mashed Potatoes, 135
Vinaigrette
    Blackberry-Honey Vinaigrette, for Baby Greens, 96
    Champagne Vinaigrette, for Butter Lettuce & Endive Salad, 91
    Cider Vinaigrette, for Gala Apple, Blue Cheese & Toasted Pecan Salad, 87
    Cranberry Vinaigrette, for Seasonal Greens, 90
    Lemon Vinaigrette, for Shaved Fennel & Arugula Salad, 81
    White Wine Vinaigrette, for Crab Towers, 65
    See also Salad dressing
Walnuts
    Brussels Sprouts with Toasted Walnut Butter, 141
    Spicy Walnuts, for Seasonal Greens, 88
Wasabi
    Wasabi Cream Cheese, for Smoked Salmon, 68
    Wasabi Mashed Potatoes, 135
Wine
    Juicy Strawberry Pineapple Sangría, 40
    Red Wine Glaze, for Seared Lamb, 123
    Winter Spiced White Wine, 35
Won tons
    Shrimp Won Ton Soup with Lemongrass, 86
Zabaglione
    Fluffy Vin Santo Zabaglione, for Fresh Berries, 178
Zesting citrus, 25
Zucchini
    Cumin-Grilled Zucchini with Tomato-Corn Summer Salsa, 143

ABOUT THE PHOTOGRAPHER

E. Jane Armstrong's celebrated food photography has appeared in a number of cookbooks, including *The Perfect Match: Pairing Delicious Recipes with Great Wine; Omelettes, Souffles and Frittatas; Pacific Northwest: The Beautiful Cookbook; Texas: The Beautiful Cookbook;* and the best-selling *Super Smoothies.* She is a twice-nominated Julia Child Cookbook Awards nominee. Armstrong's work has appeared in national magazines such as *Condé Nast Traveler* and *Food & Wine,* and she also shoots for an international roster of clients. Armstrong lives and works in Seattle.

ABOUT THE AUTHOR

Kathy Casey is celebrated as a frontrunner chef—paving the way for the emergence of women chefs and Northwest cuisine on a national level. Owner of her own company, Kathy Casey Food Studios®, she focuses on concept and menu development for restaurants and food companies nationwide, and also conducts cooking classes for the public. Casey and her cuisine have been featured in numerous national publications including *Self, Cheers, Food & Wine, Food Arts,* the *San Francisco Chronicle,* the *New York Times,* and the *Boston Globe.* Casey, a frequent TV guest, has appeared on shows such as *Good Morning America,* TV Food Network's *Unwrapped, The Other Half, Larry King Live, CBS This Morning,* and *Northern Exposure.* You can also catch her cooking on PBS. When not in the kitchen or on the set, Seattle's cocktail and culinary diva pens the monthly column, "Dishing," for the *Seattle Times.* She has also authored *Pacific Northwest: The Beautiful Cookbook,* a Julia Child Cookbook Awards nominee, and co-authored the *Best Places Seattle Cookbook.* A trend-setter and -watcher, Casey often speaks and writes on food and beverage trends.